I WANTED
TO QUIT TOO

Also by the Author:

Life is Sad and Beautiful

I WANTED
TO QUIT TOO

Stories For The Heart And Soul

Hussain Manawer

First published in Great Britain in 2024 by Hodder Catalyst
An imprint of Hodder & Stoughton
An Hachette UK company

2

A CIP catalogue record for this title is available from the British Library

Hardback ISBN 9781399705806
ebook ISBN 9781399705813

Typeset in Celeste by Hewer Text UK Ltd, Edinburgh
Printed and bound in Great Britain by Clays Ltd, Elcograf S.p.A.

Hodder & Stoughton policy is to use papers that are natural, renewable
and recyclable products and made from wood grown in sustainable
forests. The logging and manufacturing processes are expected to
conform to the environmental regulations of the country of origin.

Hodder & Stoughton Ltd
Carmelite House
50 Victoria Embankment
London EC4Y 0DZ

www.hoddercatalyst.co.uk

Dearest Ammi Jaan,

It's been six long, tiring, crying, trying, years without you by my side. I honestly don't know how I have managed. Then I must remind myself, I came from you. I was born from your love, life experiences, pain, passion, power, and Barking and Dagenham energy. With that in mind, I somehow still find ways to include you within every rhyme. Multiple times Mum, I felt the need to give up, I quite frankly wanted to die. I had no value for this thing people call life. But that's not the answer, that's not what this is, and that is not how you raised me, so on in the night, I write.

Recently Mum, people have shown me love, they have welcomed me into their homes, they have fed me, heard me, understood me and given me a place to rest my overthinking head. I then begin to feel guilty, guilty for moving on without you, but then I must remind myself I am never without you. You are within me as much as I hope and pray to convince myself I am within you.

My tears are less now, but the quantity of them never overrides their weight. My outbursts too are far and few as somehow I have developed coping mechanisms to live in this world without hearing your voice, feeling your touch, listening to you speak or being in the presence of your warmth.

I feel the air Mum, and for once it is light. My smile is real, my laugh no longer disingenuous. I am opening my heart and my arms to those who are doing so for me and in return I believe through your love and through your grief I have another chance of life. Many strong-willed, huge-hearted, passion-fuelled, incredibly fascinating people navigated into my life since you left. That's what we are doing here, right now. Creating a space, to share, to listen and to try our best to understand, connect, to emphasise in an attempt to hope to be as compassionate as we can be. Thank you Mum, for everything, even the lessons you have taught me through grief.

Forever Yours
Hussain x

My Dua (Prayer) is with you for life.

Mum
1968–2017
x

Prince Eesa
Princess Ayah
Prince Zakariya
Prince Mustafa

Contents

Part Three: Hope

CONTENTS

Part Five: Healing

Tonight I'll Cry

Dad called my phone
Said u better get home
I thought I knew pain
But here it comes tenfold

I can never really let go
Of what i'm about to tell you
The night and how it flowed
I saw hell, and I just fell through

Blue lights, police and for my mum *there's an ambulance?!*
I can't let you go, this isn't this part of the story isn't fabolous
Sudden trauma
Accidents
All I feel is . . .
Anxiousness
My mind in a paralysis
Praying for something miraculous

Your looking beautiful, mum,
Your not even wearing makeup
And there doing CPR
Ammi jaan,
You need to wake up

They got shoes up on our carpet
This is ludacris, stand up

I had no idea of where the story was about take us

A young paramedic looked at me and said:

We need to announce the time of death, I said, time
*   of death? What could it have been?*
It could be anything between a brain haemorrhage or
*   cardiac arrest*

This is everything I ever dred
wat your really telling me is,
The angels walked outta heaven
And i got stabbed with their jagged edge

I start screaming all around me,
I break down i start to cry
My mother just died her spirit must be in the sky

Which way are they taking you?!
Mum, Are you alright?!

But wait,
What am I meant to do for the rest of my life?

You never saw me get married
You never saw my have a child
You never saw us fix things
You never saw us reconcile
You never saw me break a leg
And from today, i guess what hurts the most is

You'll never see me break a smile
It's the morning of your funeral
Somehow your still looking beautiful
I don't know what to do
I don't know a feeling that's suitable

I got mud all on my trainers,
In my nails and on my hands

Burying you
Buried me

All i am, is just a man

Who's fighting with grief and its battles
It baffles and it hassles
channels as it rattles
shatters and it tackles
grapples as it unravels
Loads itself in barrels
Locks me in it's target, when i'm running from my problems,
    it shoots me on my travels

I live alone
Sleep alone
By the river and its freezing

Listening to Leona,
love is really bleeding

pain got me in a headlock
yeah it's really beating

My body its battering
For some reason it's never leaving

I tell my best friend
There's way too much to factor in
That's why
I can't turn up to there gatherings
my mind there really hammering
I'm not even in the continent
I can still hear them chattering

You see evil eye
That thing is such a weapon
I shot for the stars
And landed
in depression

Me against my mind
Stuck in armageddon
we're still fighting on the street
Why did my generation have to franchise Tekken?

nothing can facilitate
All the pain that i exhilarate
Nothing ever indicates
That hope will come accelerate
My emotions when they fluctuate
Because it's a long night,
when depression comes and dominates

i'm overwhelmed
in overdraft

The clouds above,
they over cast
My demons working overtime
I thought there was a job crisis, how are these lot
    overstaffed?
I'm from the lower cast
of the working class
This punch does really ever last
I can't look at pictures,
I get PTSD from photographs

selling me dreams
I didn't know what i was buying

i've cried myself to sleep
Guess who woke up crying

I felt all this love
And i still felt like dying

But i'm still here trying
Mummy's boy still writing

You aint robin me,
or making me doubt, fire
I got the drive in the triumph,
i'll still spit fire
Another mountain there higher
When it's all still dire
The DNA of my trauma,
i'm just tryna rewire

Faith in my spirit
Love in my bones
How have i still got
Hope in my art
When I have
hell in my home?

In the interviews,
I set the tone with my soul
I can't get no satisfaction

I'm an east london rolling stone

tonight i'll cry . . .

Introduction

As I write this to you, it's my twenty-ninth birthday. While to many of you reading this, my age is a sign of my youth and not a mark on the world. I understand that my mother was married, running a family with three children at twenty-nine. And here you have it, the birth place of my own creation of self-sabotage, which ultimately leads to me wanting to quit each and every time a thought collides with the comparison framework I have voluntarily constructed in my life.

I am not sure if it is something that the world we now live in has branded me, or if it's the teenage labels of being an underachiever, but I feel as if I have to achieve something of great magnitude every single day, just to survive in my mind. I used to view this as having a 'great work rate' and 'high productivity'. I now see this as me going to war with myself and one battle that needs to be far removed and extradited from my life.

Every time I acknowledge myself; my achievements, body, feelings, outlook, perspective, trauma, grief, knowledge, ability and capability, it only ever leads to one thing and that is, dissatisfaction. Which creates a huge forever-growing to-do list mentally, carrying with it an insane amount of pressure, forever endings of unhappiness, discontent and a harmful relationship with my mental health.

While delving deeper into depression it took me a fair few years to realise I was unable to navigate out of a place I did not want to be. Submerging my mind into darkness, I began to allow depression to control me by default, even when I am living and trying my best to be present in the magical moments of my wildest dreams.

I had to have a real conversation and ask myself, when did the inner workings of my mind get so tangled and become poisonous, when did I start working against me?

Why did I become obsessed with being a fixer for others and not myself?

What hole was I trying to fill with accomplishments?

Why were achievements falling further into an abyss and holding no weight in the silence of the night?

Why didn't I care about me?

Towards my late twenties, close friends and family members were building lives for themselves – marriages, children, homes, new foundations and beginnings. The self-isolation kicked in, I felt further and further apart from who I was once, even though I hadn't changed.

I thought career aspirations and goals would satisfy me; for a moment they did, but that doesn't sustain. I don't think it ever will. As long as I am not happy within, nothing will bring any form of peace.

I didn't know how to create a personal life for myself. All I do is sit at my desk and write all the time. It takes a lot for me to get up and move away from the seat of being commander of the spaceship. But truth be told, I gave up on myself. I had quit. And it was for a myriad of reasons. I believed I wasn't worthy of love. I think somewhere my insecurities found steroids, injected themselves and completely dominated my head, heart and any vessel that would try to intervene.

I cried and I cried for years, over countless nights, I was broken, hopeless and lost. The grief of my mum, the lack of how

I wanted to be feeling, the comparisons of destruction on social media, the whole deluxe package of depression. It had absolutely riddled me numb.

Present day: I am taking care of myself physically and in return psychologically becoming healthier too.

I can now wholeheartedly say to all of you, yes, there have been many times I Wanted To Quit Too, and still to this very day there are many moments where I feel too and in my cases I clearly did. But I've managed to develop a better ecosystem around my mental health and wellbeing, one that stops me from going to zero to self-sabotage within minutes.

I'm thirty-two now, and this took me years to adopt and install within my life. And I would be lying if I was to say to you I did it myself. It really does take an entire community group of loving, caring, understanding people to really lift you and help create a space for you to learn to love who you are becoming from the pain that you believed defined you. And also tell you the harsh truth when needed (gosh we had some dramas). It really does take a village.

Which then leads me to this book, when I was having conversations with people, honest and upfront, emotional and deep I found that there is no way I can keep all of this information to myself.

It's fair to say this book holds an immense amount of pain down its spine, strength of character within its chapters and fighting love within each of its pages.

It was birthed from heartache, frustration and this feeling of being lonely. It was also created (I had no idea at the time) as a battle tool to confront all the demons of depression and as a shield from the storms that come with trauma and armour to protect you as weaponry from the worry of uncertainties of the future. It's art-tillery, like what I did there?

And from this point, it departs my heart to find yours.

Me and Sinéad Harnett had this idea together, so thank you Sinéad, for allowing me to take the reins on this, for trusting me and for inspiring me and the world with your music, for the long talks, the hikes in Los Angeles, the manifestation sessions and every other bit of joy you bring into my life. Can you believe all them years ago when I slid into your DMs and asked you to be a part of the mental health lesson it would lead to this?

Soon it will be time for you to hear from the people I am exceptionally fortunate to have met in this journey of life who have kindly opened up for us to not only learn from but to be inspired by.

It was within these stories, conversations and moments I learnt first-hand about the dynamic power of a four-letter word called hope. The charming chaos of audacity, the risk required for when looking into taking a chance and the heart space essential to be optimistic. The expense of love, which if true, one day will lead you and hand you over to the guardians at the gates of grief.

I learnt of the punishment the child within us faces for holding on to ambition. The distraction of desire along with the desire of distraction, the importance of failure, the beauty inside the walls of procrastination, the heartbreak that follows heartbreak. The losses that come with success, the price we stop and pay by the toll charge on the road to destiny, how hurt unknowingly transforms to become life experience and that health and culture sometimes clash.

I learnt that the need to challenge can be done compassionately, that there is a human need to hold on to passion, how family is a universal concept and that many traditions hold significant purpose and must be protected.

I learnt that not all needs are needy and that not all wealth is rich, that money in many cases can bring happiness. That sadness needs its time to be sad, but never let that feeling overstay its welcome.

I learnt that regardless of the evils in the way the mind has an innate ability to strategically manoeuvre to a healthier place.

That odds can be defied while you are unaware, that stigma can be demystified, taboo can be addressed and put on display as art, that trauma stands no chance against talent, that depression is hopeless vs conversation and the mighty power of the gut will reveal the truth in an attempt to save the day.

I learnt through all of these stories that growth one day meets evolution, which eventually finds peace and beholds wisdom.

That through all life brings, if we have the capacity to imagine, if we have the safety to try, the ability to develop, the privilege to step forward then we really can and we really should change the world we live in today for the better.

I learnt that breaking down leads to breaking in and eventually to breaking through.

Within the stories of *I Wanted to Quit Too* I learnt through cross-generations, through different cultures, lifestyles and life experiences, through parallel universes and worlds, the exceptional essence of wanting to give up and the true power and magic behind, or should I say in front of, never doing so.

This book was compiled for you, it was created as a lifeline, a best friend in the pages, a hug in the words for those of us who feel misunderstood and discouraged, for everyone who can't seem to make sense as to why it's not working, for everyone who dreams and feels a world away from their destiny, for those who feel they are too old to start now, for each of us who keeps going not knowing where it will go, for every one of us who dares to get up and make something out of the heartbreak and heartache of our lives, for every one of us not knowing love, affection, care, touch, warmth, for every one of us who packs our entire lives into small little suitcases to travel away from the small little towns we came from to chase our dreams within huge polluted cities, for every one of us who is paying the ultimate sacrifice of ambition, the excruciating cost of aspiration, for every one of us who is simply trying to get through another day of life. This is for you.

It was never a dream of mine to put together a book as special, precious, fragile and powerful as this, but it's important, it's very important.

To all the contributors who participated, thank you from the bottom of my heart for firstly being in my life. You have all in many ways been incredibly supportive to me, thank you for lending your words, your teachings, guidance, wisdom, love and blessings and most of all your names to the *I Wanted To Quit Too* anthology.

Now, with all the pleasure, passion and power in my beating little heart,

Drum roll please

I am so fortunate to welcome you to our book, the collection, the literary voyage (I'm dramatic, I know), the anthology that is . . .

I WANTED TO QUIT TOO.

'There's always a rhyme at the end of the tunnel.'
— Doctor Poetry

Opening Statement
ANONYMOUS

And the high priests came down from the mountain.

People don't decide to be Kings and Queens. They are ordained, chosen, or . . .

They must carve themselves through determination and spirit and the will to do good.

To be wise is to know great failures and victories, to have experienced all and to have made every mistake in the book.

And to remain resilient in the face of adversity, unflinching, kind and non-judgemental. But hold the space. For the waves that come next and stitch the community.

Together bind the generations. In unity.

When the veil of illusion is ripped we cannot stitch it back together.

We must find a way to navigate this unpredictable landscape that can be hostile and most joyful with our eyes open.

Much we have learned of medicine and healing has come
from the battlefield, battlefield surgery and pain relief.
alchemists aside. Remedies sourced. Provided in the
constitution of the earth and its rich resources. The high
priests and priestesses. Shamans and the spiritual empaths,
psychics – and clerics.

The warriors having spent their time on the battlefield
negotiating the unknown, the unpredictable and the
four horsemen – knew how close traversing their mortality
was daily.

And time served there perhaps brought with it
something spiritual.

They coped and carried their wounds until they could no
longer move forward in their old ways and thus in time some
Found sanctuary in the cathedral –

And in healing
The witness of experiences of life and death
And the uncanny happening

Forced them to be awake
Is nothing but spiritual

The warriors welcomed other warriors in the sanctuary
Identified their own and their need
Humanity
From battles passed and now into this time
now of reflection
Of then of passing on

And as the warrior levelled then came with it
the sad monk and the feminine strength
And the integration of these three forged Kings
and Queens of them all.

Who learned to rule by wisdom
Of the years experienced
From tending the wounds they had inflicted on others
and ultimately themselves – in healing
found connection with the earth, love for one another
and all creatures

The hope of brutal learnings the optimism of the initiated
The pursuit of noble intention and decency

To payback into community
For service and leadership

The joy of healing of tending wounds from the
understanding of their infliction and then giving back

And they rolled it all back in. To serve the new generation
who had their battles yet to come.

Without judgement the elders held the space for
youthful folly and warriorship.

Courage to dare.

Allowed the space to make mistakes and leave each
other to their own decision making.

But as one moved forward unified by a care that goes beyond the superficial.

And the tip of the spear stayed sharp and deft and adaptable because the purpose behind this tool was there.

To hold close and protect those humanities and those that struggled in the pursuit of good and nobility and integrity and faced the changes that were always inevitable for them.

On their road.

What Is A Poetry Slam?
ANONYMOUS

It's ...
... when poets compete
in a number of heats
with a few minutes each
during which to try and reach
the hearts and minds
of those discerning kinds
who hear what they say
and respond in their own way
with tears or cheers
laughter or applause
with cries of encore
or a silent pause

judges judge how the audience reacts
it's competitive and lively and some might say perhaps
it's a bit like the Booker
because occasionally you find that some crazy ...
... poet emerges as the winner who is not
a slam champ but just a brave beginner
who has the guts to stand right up
and stand and deliver
a stanza that captures
the moment and enraptures
those who are there

it's poetry in motion
it's poetry in yer face
it's the spoken word spoken
with power panache and pace
it's sharp it's loose
it's tender it's mean
it's poets being heard
it's poets being seen
town hall next friday 8.15

be there

Welcome In
SINÉAD HARNETT

Singer, songwriter, friend

Growing up I wish I had a book like this to read. One to tell me it's gonna be okay. One to offer me the love and support I so desperately craved.

Truth is, no matter where you come from, you deserve to fight for your dreams as much as anybody else.

Our light can frighten us. We wonder if we deserve to shine. We think, *'Who am I to assume others will like me and what I have to offer?'* But light is there to be seen, and it belongs inside us all.

I can't tell you the amount of times I thought I'd give up. Life is a funny old thing. One minute you've cracked it and the next you feel more lost than you did to start with. But fully surrendering to my calling, simply for the love of it, has always kept me climbing the mountain.

Depression, anxiety and OCD-thinking have been close friends of mine, but dealing with my trauma in therapy has really helped me bat away thoughts of quitting. I think once I realised that writing music was my best offering to the world, instead of letting it be such a failure test in my head, helped me to keep going.

So whatever it is you feel you want to do, even if heading towards that or discovering it takes baby steps, please ... GO! May as well give it a try while we're here.

And maybe you'll have a laugh along the way. Laughter is pretty fantastic.

All my love, Sinéad x

PART ONE

Health

DAME TIL WYKES
LOLA YOUNG
PAULA NAUGHTON
ANNIKA WAHEED
LOUISE HILL-DAVIS
REN GILL
NIAH SELWAY
LARRY LAMB
KEVIN HINES
ANONYMOUS
DAN DARE
SONNA RELE
HUSSAIN MANAWER
SURFING SOFAS

No Health Without Mental Health

DAME TIL WYKES

Professor of Clinical Psychology and Rehabilitation, Institute of Psychiatry, Psychology and Neuroscience, King's College London and the South London and Maudsley NHS Foundation Trust

Life contains bumps and sometimes mountains that get in the way and can cause us to lose control, forget our coping skills, deliver low moods and occasionally a downward spiral so deep the future disappears. This section of the book contains some heart-warming and heart-rending stories of trauma, physical disability and illness. It is a celebration of the survivors who learn to value themselves and who are speaking up about the time and effort that takes.

Our healthcare system is not invincible and is sometimes the problem. If you rely on test results and textbooks, a diagnosis or just a helpful treatment will be elusive. That challenge has affected several contributors, who found the waiting time altered their life completely. Diagnosis was also not the end of the heartache as there's grief in a diagnosis as it can mean a complete review of life chances.

Our authors also showed great courage in overcoming the barriers to recovery from both physical and mental illness. All showing that with baby steps they can move forward, recognising their hard-won successes but also telling us that this doesn't happen overnight.

People now talk about a big word – resilience. It is as if this is built into our genes or somehow the lack of it means we are vulnerable and lacking in key pieces of the human jigsaw. Some authors built a repertoire of coping strategies, learning from

3

trial and error when and what they need to do. These skirmishes with our thoughts sometimes produce a 'levelling up' even when we are on the losing side. Others, and it is a bigger group, tell us that they relied on other people because inner strength develops through support from a much wider community.

What can we learn from the pages ahead? That mental health problems can be the result of life's trials or can just be bad luck linked to your DNA. They can also result in ill health. Our research has shown that physical and mental health are linked. Depression following a heart attack can increase the chance of a second one and the outcomes for asthma and rheumatoid arthritis.

Aneurin Bevan, founder of the NHS, said, 'Illness is neither an indulgence for which people have to pay, nor an offence for which they should be penalised, but a misfortune the cost of which should be shared by the community.' So, resilience isn't just personal; it is about how your community supports you. That's why talking about mental health problems is important; it helps reduce discrimination and stigma as well as allowing us to provide support where it is needed.

Words can be helpful (and hurtful) – you choose. Ask someone, 'Are you okay?' and they will probably say 'fine'. If you follow up with 'Out of ten, what would you score yourself today?' then you may discover the real meaning of 'fine'. We can all help someone who is struggling, just by listening, and that support can be vital.

Looking back, I can see that I have used many conflict words in this introduction – battles, skirmishes, challenges and struggles. As Taylor Swift said to graduating students at New York University, 'My mistakes led to the best things in my life . . . dusting yourself off and seeing who wants to hang out is a gift . . . those moments were as important or more crucial.'

Making a mistake or losing a battle is part of the lifelong human experience. What I have learnt from our courageous contributors is that learning to cope, developing strength, confidence and self-worth is a marathon not a sprint.

T Is For Trauma

LOLA YOUNG

Artist, poet, friend

T is for trauma
I know what she looks like
I've held her with my own two hands
Sometimes she looks like a disease other times like a daisy
She cuts like a bullet but sings like a bird
And Sometimes i pray to her
Other times i pretend she doesn't exist
She is pretty, i pity the sight of me when she walks in,

She sleeps in the cracks in my walls, seeps through the ache in
my chest, tells me i can't do this, then tells me i can, i wonder
how far she's travelled when she holds my breath, and i have
been holding my breath my whole life.

I know what she looks like, I've painted over her with laughter,
I have sunk my teeth into her when I can't chew, I have held
her in light and in darkness, high as the moon, fumbling for
patience and peace and occasionally wishing that she would
say 'you'll be fine without me'

Go Home And Love Your Children
PAULA NAUGHTON

Mother, wife, nurse, advocate, miracle seeker

Friday 9 November 2012

As we sat in the consulting room with our beautiful two-year-old cherubic twins George and Isaac, I felt more terrified than on any other occasion in my life. Two days previously our three beautiful sons had visited this hospital to have blood tests and we were here to get the results.

To distract myself I tried to picture our beautiful eldest son Archie. He was seven years old and currently at school, totally unaware of the landmine that our family was about to jump on. I imagined him laughing; Archie was always laughing because he was filled with joy and adventure. His existence equalled unbridled happiness and fun despite the enormous challenges he had already overcome in his short life. As I sat there I was instantly transported back to April 2008 as we had run onto this very ward carrying our semi-conscious two-year-old son. I had just had a massive fight with a paediatric SHO in A & E after he labelled me hysterical because I refused to take Archie home, instead demanding to see a paediatric nurse. Just as we arrived at the doors of the Paediatric High Dependency Unit Archie lost consciousness. The next morning Dr Galvin,* the consultant, came to tell us that the next 24–72 hours were crucial. The theory was that Archie had pneumonia. If that was not frightening enough, it later transpired he had pneumonia, bacterial meningitis and septicaemia. Days later the courageous and heroic baby boy woke up; apart from a slight limp on his left leg he was unscathed. It was an absolute miracle.

The door swung open and the noise brought me abruptly back to now. A very dejected-looking man walked into the room. Having spent considerable time with him when Archie was so ill, I knew; I knew he was carrying an enormous and unwelcome burden with him. I was also 99 per cent certain of what he was going to tell us. In fact I was so confident that I had shared my thoughts with my lovely husband the previous night. Not unlike the SHO four years previously, Padraic labelled me hysterical. His own theory was that God would never allow all three of our sons to be so ill. He reasoned that it made no sense, especially because as nurses we had both spent our entire professional lives helping people. I prayed all night that he was right and that I was indeed hysterical.

Dr Galvin welcomed us. I felt so sorry for him. Dear Lord, what an awful job. I wanted to take away his unease and, dare I say, his pity for us; it was etched into his face. All of these thoughts had raced through my brain and he had only said hello. I could feel a pain in my chest and Padraic and I held on to each other instinctively; as if somehow this might shield us from what was to come. By this stage George and Isaac were fast asleep; their glowing pink cheeks and slow steady breaths brought a few seconds of relief as I gazed at them.

Then he began. 'I am so sorry to tell you that the three boys all have muscular dystrophy.' Armed with my limited Dr Google knowledge, I asked, 'Is it DMD?'

'I am afraid so, Paula.'

At this stage I had an out-of-body experience. For a moment I did actually wonder if I had died; I was looking down on everyone from above. I could hear muffled voices and I noticed that Padraic had turned grey. I felt as though I was floating for hours. I saw all the hopes and dreams we had for our magnificent sons evaporate and wondered how many valleys we would fill with tears following this life-changing revelation.

You see, DMD is short for Duchenne Muscular Dystrophy. It is a catastrophic muscle-wasting disease that has no treatment or cure. It mainly affects boys and its natural trajectory means that between the ages of eight and twelve years, children lose the ability to walk. During their teenage years, if they live that long, they continue to get physically weaker. They lose upper body strength and the ability to move their arms. This means they cannot do all the basic things the rest of us take for granted, such as feeding themselves, brushing their teeth or even scratching their nose. If that wasn't horrific enough, the muscles that control breathing as well as the heart muscle are also damaged. Consequently boys die of respiratory and/or cardiac failure. The average life expectancy is nineteen to twenty-two years of age.**

As I floated back into the chair next to Padraic, I heard myself thinking, this cannot happen. They cannot have Duchenne. Duchenne is a terminal illness. Archie wants to be a rugby player and play soccer for Chelsea. George wants to be a chef and Isaac wants to be a bin man.

'I am so sorry this has happened to you both.' I heard Padraic say thank you to Dr Galvin for his kindness and then heard myself reply, 'But it hasn't happened to us has it, it has happened to Archie, George and Isaac.' The room fell silent. Before we left we were advised that there is hope with research that treatments might be developed in the coming years. We were also told that an appointment would be sent to us to see the national expert in the coming weeks.

We walked to the car in silence. On the journey home I suggested to Padraic that we kill ourselves and the boys there and then. He agreed that this was an option, only for us to remember that Archie was still at school and we could not possibly leave him. We drove to school to collect our handsome son knowing he would be grinning from ear to ear to see all four of us greet him.

Monday 12 November 2012

We went to work. Archie went to school and George and Isaac spent the day with Caroline, their beautiful childminder. We both wanted to die but made the decision that morning that quitting was not an option.

Monday 21 January 2013

The place was like a maze; was this really the centre of excellence that we had been promised? A porter turned us back from the entrance and told us we needed to go out of the building and take a different lift to the top floor. It was not a good start but we were hopeful that things would improve. As always Archie, George and Isaac took everything in their stride and were chatting to each other and laughing. They are just such a joy. Pure magic.

Once we finally reached the correct clinic we had to fill in some forms. Following this the boys had to be weighed and their height measured and have their vital signs recorded. We were then led into a room to meet the consultant. He asked about each of the boys individually and then examined them in turn. Following this a nurse took them to the play room.

This was my opportunity.

I pulled out pages of information I had collected over the past two months. I had contacted paediatric neurologists, scientists and pharmaceutical companies all over the world. I had many email conversations with them and numerous telephone discussions too. They were all so passionate about their work. They had filled me with the hope that Dr Galvin had told us about and I was excited to have this validated by the national expert. He was very kind and listened to me for some time as I waxed lyrical about micro-dystrophin research in London, France and the USA as well as tonnes of other studies. I told him we were going to raise money for research in the hope of making clinical trials an option for every child diagnosed with Duchenne.

I asked him what he thought.

It was at this point that he put his head in his hands. He then looked up and said, 'Padraic and Paula, the best advice I can give you is to go home and love your children.'

It is impossible to articulate how betrayed we felt. We do not need a doctor to tell us to love our children; we do love our children!! We need a solution. We need to save the lives of our sons and all the other children.

We now realise that we have a new life. Our old life, BD (Before Duchenne), has gone forever. We somehow have to embrace this new existence that we refer to as AD (After Duchenne). The monster that is Duchenne cannot be allowed to steal our magnificent sons; how can anyone expect any parents to bury their three children?

See www.joinourboys.org for more information.

* Dr Galvin is a pseudonym.

** 2012 figures.

Hormones And Heartache

ANNIKA WAHEED

Women's health advocate

For nearly two years, a bit of me chipped away every cycle. By cycle I mean my menstrual cycle. You know the thing that nobody talks about? Your whole life you were told to hide your pads when you needed to be excused to go to the ladies' room, or nobody in the household could know you were menstruating.

'Periods can't make you feel like this can they?'
Make you feel like what?
Like I wanted to die.

Like when I couldn't get out of the car in the car park at work because I was having an anxiety attack.

Like when I would disappear for two weeks of the month at a time and not talk to Jihan, my bestie and soul mate, when usually we would talk nearly every day despite her living in Holland.

Like when I would cry uncontrollably like someone died for no reason. Maybe someone did. I did. For two weeks of the month at a time. Every time. Every month without fail.

Like the dysphoria where I couldn't recognise my reflection in the mirror, when I didn't leave my bed for three days without showering or brushing my teeth.

Like the soul behind my eyes disappeared.

Like when I'd hope that I would get hit by a bus instead of feeling the sense of nothingness and dread, the dysphoria.

Like feeling I'm existing and not living.

Like the colour of the world disappearing.

Like when I had endless assignments to mark at work and would stare at the screen because I couldn't concentrate.

Like when I had brain fog.

Like when I had an insatiable appetite and couldn't stop eating, hoping it would take the pain away.

Like when I either slept too much or had insomnia waiting for the night to take me away from it all.

Like when my body felt so heavy and lethargic that it was like I had two large boulders tied to my feet.

Like despair. Complete, utter despair.

Like when my world ended for me every month, every few weeks, every cycle, every year for a few years. Only to be resurrected again when my period began.

My period did that all to me?

No, my love, your body's response to the hormonal fluctuations after you begin to ovulate does this to you.

The menstruation bleed, the period, the one I had been told to hide, disguise and is dirty. Is the same thing that gave me relief from the torment for weeks on end.

'But Doctor, I don't feel like myself for weeks on end – why do I suffer immensely before my period?'

'Your bloods and scans are fine – are you sure you're not stressed? Why don't you try for a baby?'

Nervous breakdown 1.0 in November 2019. The intensity and dysphoria was too much. I'm feeling everything and nothing all at the same time.

It's been fourteen days. I can't do this any more. I'm tired. So, so, tired.

One overdose and twenty-three minutes of violently vomiting later. 'I can't keep doing this on my own any more.'

I wanted to quit. Taking that overdose screamed to quit.

I couldn't.

Mental health crisis line: *So it's like P . . . M . . . S?*

It's not f***** PMS. It's PMS's satanic sibling – PMDD.

I'm sharing my story. I won't be shamed for screaming about a disorder that medical professionals are supposed to know or help us women with. It's unbelievably lonely when in a state of dysphoria. I promised myself I don't want another woman to go through what I did. GPs have never heard of it. Gynaecologists don't care about it. Mental health rejected it.

I wanted to quit.

What the hell do I do now?

Fight the imposter syndrome, my love. You know more than the professionals. Talk about it. Don't stop talking about it, babe. Tell the world that you'll take those antidepressants without it being tainted with shame for when your serotonin falls after ovulation. Tell the world you can make it work with your career and coexist with the demonic disorder.

Hormones and Heartache is born.

Take the HRT. The hormone replacement therapy that society tells you that only 'old women' take.

Utilise your resources working for the NHS. Use your talent and natural ability to teach the medical professionals.

I got this message the other day and it made all the fighting and writing worthwhile . . .

'Annika, I started taking antidepressants after watching you talk so openly about it on Instagram. I have a three-year-old. I no longer want to throw myself under the bus for the first time in years – thank you! Please don't stop sharing your story – you've helped my daughter have her mum.'

Gas & Air

LOUISE HILL-DAVIS

Facilitator and performance artist
(from her, to me, to you)

Have you ever shared your aspirations of becoming a
performance artist with a Nigerian mother? Lauren did.

Lauren, a Londoner of Nigerian and Jamaican descent, had
experienced the loss of her father during her childhood. This
instilled in her the understanding that life is precious and
fleeting. Lauren's mother was a first-generation immigrant.
Higher education was non-negotiable. So, Lauren attended
university during the day and performed at night. When she
finally earned her degree, her mother beamed with pride. She
was going to be somebody someday.

Being a 5ft 9 Black woman from East London, and a size 20,
Lauren never quite fitted into her small town of Fordwich. The
move made her smaller, quieter, and *'lovely'*. Her ability to code-
switch had improved, although her mother would occasionally
remind her that she didn't need to use that voice at home.
Lauren started dating one of her friends, a kind man with a
good family. However, he wasn't Nigerian, nor was he Black.
This fact held significance within her community. Although
she couldn't articulate it, she knew it meant something in his
community too.

When Lauren's mother passed away, Lauren wore her
mother like a shield. She walked like her, talked like her, and
ran the family business as if it were her own dream. Grief
visited her at night. She drank. She smoked. She fought with

demons of her past reminding her of who she was. She was haunted by a parallel life – one filled with risks, rebellion and recklessness. She pushed those thoughts aside, exchanging them for Christian values and a simple narrative of a nuclear family.

Within a year Lauren found herself pregnant and unmarried, searching for a place to live.

'Tani mos ṣẹ.'

Her boyfriend agreed to marry her, but she felt a deep sense of shame. At three months pregnant they hastily arranged a wedding, keeping the whole truth from her family. The rushed preparations left little room for speculation. Six months later Lauren was heavily pregnant and overdue. Unfortunately, she was often dismissed and sent home when she mentioned pain, lack of movement or fatigue. A part of her wanted to prove she could handle this alone, to embody the strong Black women she admired on TV. She confided in her close friend Frieda, who explained that the vulnerability that came with childbirth was unlike anything she had experienced before. Frieda strongly advised that someone, anyone, be with Lauren at the hospital because Frieda didn't know if she would have survived without her mum by her side. Lauren said nothing.

Finally, the moment arrived. Her partner was by her side as a witness to the horror that unfolded. After enduring twelve hours of labour, a long needle was inserted to rupture the amniotic sac. The water revealed the presence of meconium. Lauren relied on gas and air for pain relief. With every inhale she drew in hope, reassurance and anticipation. Her daughter was on her way. Each exhale brought a harsh reality – pain, and a sense of emptiness. Becoming a mother when your own mother has passed away is an agonising journey. By the nineteenth hour, something felt wrong. The epidural had failed multiple times, and Lauren was exhausted. She began to give up, to let go.

It was a Monday morning, 7.30 a.m., when the consultant arrived. Urgent measures were taken. Another midwife and a healthcare assistant entered. Lauren's legs were placed in stirrups, and she was asked to sign something while her partner stood by her head. Everything happened so rapidly. One person restrained each leg, and two others positioned themselves between them. The consultant briefly explained the situation to Lauren – she had progressed too far, and pain relief was no longer an option. They had to perform an episiotomy without anaesthetic. Holding her legs down, they made the incision. Lauren left her body and begged God to stop the pain. She cried a broken cry as her body pushed against the professionals restraining her legs in the stirrups. Blood gushed from the incisions as the midwife and consultant called for more light. Multiple cuts were made. The consultant struggled to see. Panic filled the room. Death was near. Lauren was ordered to push. Push!

Finally, her baby arrived. Liquid life left her body. The midwife called for a transfusion and administered localised anaesthetic. All she could do was sing with gratitude, thanking her deity for putting her back in her body with her daughter in her arms.

Due to the trauma, Lauren required additional days in the hospital. Eventually it was time to go home with her husband and daughter. They spent a few nights together as a family before he left for work. Lauren's aunties provided traditional Nigerian post-partum healing remedies. She tightly wrapped her waist with a wrapper, sat on a commode filled with hot boiled water and Dettol for ten minutes to remove impurities, and enjoyed a capful of gin (her favourite) every three days.

After the first week the aunties left, and her godmother stayed for a night. It was then that Lauren's condition began to deteriorate. Her skin grew pale and damp, and she was slow to respond. Concerned, her godmother called a GP. No actions were taken. Lauren shared that she had passed a blood clot larger than a 50-pence coin. Frieda promptly took her to the GP, who inexplicably sent her home. That night Lauren passed a blood clot the size of a basketball. She woke up drenched in her own blood, her daughter crying in the nearby Moses basket. Lauren asked Frieda to call an ambulance.

That night Lauren believed it was her time to go. She had no fight left. She thought she was going to her final resting place. She yearned for her mother's presence. Lauren felt grateful that she had met her daughter, but she was exhausted and ready to sleep. She listened to the sirens wailing as they raced down the motorway. She closed her eyes.

Lauren woke up in the hospital. The surgery had been a success.

An infection from internal bleeding had occurred. The initial incisions made to facilitate her daughter's delivery were rushed and jagged, leading to an unorthodox stitching of the wound. Somewhere along the line, internal bleeding had taken place, causing the formation of a clot within Lauren's body. After a few more nights in the hospital, she was allowed to return home.

At work, Lauren recalled some of her experiences with other mothers. As she listened to other women share their stories, patterns emerged. White women and women of colour were having different experiences of childbirth in the NHS. The Black women from church shared that they had been dismissed, suffered infections, and sometimes felt that their physicians did not believe their pain.

Five years on, Lauren is healing – mentally and physically. She is a mother, a wife, a sister, an aunt, and each day she is more and more herself.

'We will not stay silent.'

It's important to acknowledge that the experiences described in the story are representative of real-life experiences faced by many Black women, and that the statistics regarding maternal mortality rates amongst different racial and ethnic groups are indeed a cause for concern. The healthcare disparities and systemic racism present in the healthcare system need to be addressed and actively worked upon to ensure equitable and safe care for all individuals.

It's crucial to raise awareness, advocate for change, and work towards eliminating racial disparities in healthcare. By sharing stories and shedding light on these issues, we can contribute to a broader dialogue and promote efforts to improve maternal healthcare outcomes for marginalised communities.

I Wanted My Illness To Kill Me

REN GILL

Artist

Back in 2015 when I was most ill, I hadn't gotten out of bed except when I could find the energy to shower. I was in bed for more than twenty-three hours a day. The pain was intense, a lot of dizziness along with extreme mental and physical discomfort. As my symptoms got worse I moved back in with my mum. Having had a best friend die by suicide, I didn't ever want to put that on to someone and make them wish they would have done more. What I really wanted was for my body to quit so that I was absolved of the responsibility of making that decision. If my illness killed me, it meant I didn't have to choose to die; I used to pray for that, honestly.

That was my lowest period. I was in deep, deep psychosis for a few months; I was on the sidelines of life, watching friends on social media doing things that 25-year-olds are meant to do: meeting the love of their lives, getting married, having kids, settling down, starting a family, getting jobs, all of that. I felt like I was in a state of purgatory, but worse than that, because it was almost as if I was in a torture chamber in my own body. I couldn't watch TV, read a book – these moments at my worst I really thought, what's the point of being alive to exist if it's pure suffering? Existence didn't seem worthwhile.

The internet became a source of hope I would spend so much time on it, countless hours when I had the energy. I'd search for stories of people who had overcome chronic illness, problems or impossible situations, where they'd been given a terminal diagnosis. I was actively seeking these stories out. Sometimes I'd even reach out to these people, and these stories became lifelines, buoyancy aids for me.

I wasn't willing to accept my reality. I was determined to research my way out of this. Even if it wasn't obvious with science or mainstream medicine, I was determined to find a way out and that became my place of hope.

I was diagnosed with bipolar, which later turned out to be a misdiagnosis. I was then diagnosed with ME, which also turned out to be a misdiagnosis. I kept going to the doctors and they thought that I was a hypochondriac because I'd be like, 'Look, test my blood for something different because there's something biologically wrong with me. It's not in my head like I'm hurting.'

I went for MRI scans, brain scans, I went for every blood test you can name.

Everything was always coming back negative. I got really frustrated, I visited hundreds of doctors with my physical health declining and my mental health only getting worse.

It was 2015, I was back with my mum, bed-bound for eight months before I had a psychotic breakdown. I started hallucinating. I then started thinking if I behaved in a way people didn't expect I'd short-circuit my reality, because I thought I was being watched and that my level of suffering was either due to a cruel experiment or something demonic.

This was my psychosis talking. I started doing crazy things. One time I stripped off all my clothes and I went and lay naked in the middle of a main road and started a traffic jam until the police showed up. Luckily, I wasn't sectioned for that. Then I started making everything in the house like perfectly parallel and developed this sort of stutter and tic.

There was almost a lucid part of me that was in the passenger seat watching this happen.

My behaviour patterns had traits akin to severe autism at the time. I was waking up with night terrors and screaming. My verbal communication really went downhill. But I still had this lucid part of myself.

I was looking on the internet and I found this subset of kids with autism with this condition called PANDAS (Pediatric Autoimmune Neuropsychiatric Disorders Associated with streptococcal infections), which is where the streptococcus bacteria gets into the brain. After research, I was sure this was what I had.

I convinced my mum to take me to a gastroenterologist because I had found out that if I took a course of this antibiotic, a penicillin, it targets streptococcal bacteria and it helps bring kids into remission from this subset of autism. I got myself to this gastroenterologist and I faked a stomach bug. I took the penicillin and my symptoms got rid of the psychosis. They went right down.

What I didn't know at the time was I actually had Lyme disease and what I was doing was knocking the Lyme disease bacteria down. I just had my wires slightly crossed, so I was chasing something. But the antibiotic that I took also, luckily for my sake, targeted it anyway.

This happens and then my symptoms start creeping back about a couple of weeks after the course of penicillin because it had gotten chronic at this point. I saved up money for months, my mum lent me cash and I went to see one of the best infectious disease specialists in Belgium. Before I even did the blood test, he was like, 'You've got Lyme disease, you've got all the symptoms of Lyme disease.'

He did the tests and it turned out positive for Lyme disease, which sent me on the right path to get my health back, which followed with stem cell transplants.

It was a moment of serendipity. A stroke of luck and persistence. Not giving up on the fact because I could have at that moment been like, the doctors have said I've got psychosis and there's nothing wrong with me biologically. I maybe would have ended up in a mental institution or sectioned, and that's the way I was heading. No doctor in the UK thought to test me for Lyme disease.

It was really upsetting leaving the doctors and having had some of them speak in a patronising way, with comments like, 'Oh you've been looking it up on Google, you know more than a doctor do you?'

In that moment it's really hard to hold on to hope. You can start to feel insane, you begin to doubt yourself, you're ill, you're sick, you can't keep food down, you feel this burning pain in your bones and people are telling you it's a mental condition. I had to keep coming back to this, telling myself, 'No, you're not insane.' I find it quite shocking because there's probably quite a few people who've slipped through the cracks in the system who just took the word as gospel and didn't carry on looking for answers.

I think it highlighted a real flaw in the system for people who go through either severe mental health problems or severe chronic health problems. I soon realised I was not alone in this experience.

Sometimes people go twenty years without a diagnosis. I luckily got mine eight years in. But even some people think you waited eight years for a diagnosis, they'll think that's insane.

The first year was really difficult when I started getting sick; I remember saying to my mum, I can't do another year of this,

I just can't physically or emotionally. I'm not strong enough to deal with another year. But then, another year passes and you just do, there's a survival instinct in you that allows you to get through it.

People say to me they don't think they can get through what I got through, but you can. We're incredibly adaptable to horrific situations. And there are some people who in moments opt out of that struggle. But I do think that faced with extremely horrific circumstances, humans are incredibly resilient.

For me, art is a way of justifying the suffering because it's a way of alchemising suffering into something more positive. Maybe that's a lifeboat for somebody else. These years of being trapped, suffering, allow me to draw on them as a form of expression. They probably will be an endless source for the rest of my life, an infinite source of material and inspiration, which is now manifesting in such a way that it's helping.

A lot of people feel like music doesn't represent them. Especially if it's related to a chronic health problem, there's not a lot you can relate to out there in the charts. Music gives somebody a companion, when it's difficult to find one. When I was going through it, I would have done anything to end this, I would hack off my own arm to stop this happening right now. And for me now, it gives a purpose to something that felt massively purposeless at the time.

Receiving the diagnosis was really emotional, it felt validating because for eight years I was made to feel like a hypochondriac. There was always a part of me that knew the reason why I never stopped looking and even during the psychosis I was looking. When getting the diagnosis I felt validated in a huge way.

And no way does it mean the end of the journey because after that it's like, wow, it's been misdiagnosed for so long. After that came bitterness because I'm still dealing with the consequences now of having had Lyme disease in my body for such a long time.

It's 2024 and I'm still treating autoimmunity and stuff in Canada and having to pick up the pieces. So there was a little bit of relief. And there was also a little bit of f**k, if people had just cared more or I've been educated more on this, I'd been able to save myself eight years of hell.

But you know it's a very complex multicoloured thing because also then I wouldn't have this material to draw on and I wouldn't be able to be in the position that I am in, maybe.

I felt incredibly isolated because of a lot of things. I was sick from a really early age and because I didn't have a diagnosis or I couldn't explain it, people couldn't really relate to me like, brain fog, zoning out, losing my personality, losing my energy, going from this really like sort of happy-go-lucky sort of person to like, dealing with my symptoms everyday, so I lost a lot of friends.

My family didn't understand it because my dad was a psychotherapist and he thought it was a mental health thing and he kept trying to give me advice, which kind of fell flat because I had Lyme disease. My mum was really supportive but also didn't really understand what was happening because no one could tell her what was happening. I couldn't even tell her, the doctors would tell her that I was just going through deep depression.

I felt really isolated, to be honest, and if I'm just being really honest, I actually felt pretty alienated from my friends and family.

Even now, I have to put up with symptoms. I think it justifies every moment. And I'd like to put that out there for the people who are feeling like there's no way out, because for me it was pretty impossible.

The thought of there being a way out and, for a long long time, trying to manufacture hope by seeking other people's stories. There was a huge part of me pointing out and telling myself, you're not gonna make thirty. You're gonna die before you hit thirty.

I know that the way that my life has turned out is a total 180 right now in terms of success. And people don't necessarily have to strive around and have this Cinderella story, but I want you to know the sentiment that you can turn things around even in impossible situations.

I got sick first of all in 2009, and it wasn't until probably 2017 that I started actually finding relief from those symptoms.

It was a long time, it's not always easy, but I definitely can sit here hand on heart and say it was worthwhile holding on.

The Diagnosis That Nearly Made Me Quit
NIAH SELWAY

Video creator, author and optimist

I had felt the desire to quit many times in my life, but the feeling rarely lasted longer than a few days. For years, I had defined 'quitting' as refusing to finish Question 10 on my homework or deciding to no longer see the boy I was seeing. Before my medical diagnosis, I considered 'quitting' to be *anything* I gave up on in life – even the trivial stuff. It really wasn't until I found myself in a doctor's office at seventeen years old, being diagnosed with an *allergy to water*, that I really understood what it felt like to want to quit.

As a child, I suffered from constant itching, dryness, rashes and general pain on my skin, which was always diagnosed as eczema. By the time I reached five years old, my skin had made a habit of erupting into pain shortly after I did water-based activities, like showering or swimming. Contact with water would cause an intense itching sensation, accompanied by a painful burning from underneath my skin's surface. For *years*, my doctors insisted that I was suffering from eczema and *nothing more*. So, my parents just did what they could to keep me comfortable. I remember, as a child, my mum would come by the school after my weekly swimming lessons to apply eczema cream over my body. It was the only way my skin would stand a chance of being comfortable enough for me to return to class. I spent a large portion of my childhood trying to remove potential allergens from my hygiene routine. My intuition – even back then – told me there was something *wrong*. I continued with my process of elimination, until I was eventually left with only water in my routine. Water is one of the purest things this Earth produces. How could it be hurting me? Cleansing processes like bathing, showering or even washing my hands very quickly became anxiety-inducing, as I had noticed a clear pattern. I would wash my body, then the pain would shortly follow.

As the years went on, it became clear that my skin was highly reactive when it encountered *any type of water*, including my own sweat, tears and urine. My mother had spent twelve years of my childhood fighting for an accurate diagnosis, which would often be met with suggestions that my symptoms were 'in my head' or even 'for attention'. I had spent over a decade of my childhood attending doctors' appointments, in a desperate attempt to find an explanation. So, when my symptoms were ignored, I, too, started to believe that the pain existed only *in my head*. My inner voice would tell me to 'toughen up', convincing me that water had the same effect on everyone. I believed that I was being dramatic and spent my entire childhood pretending not to be in pain.

That was until one day, after one particularly painful shower, I decided to do my bi-monthly Google search for an answer. I had done this since I had been old enough to use the internet and, each time, I thought of a new way to ask *why showers hurt me*. I would type things like 'skin hurts after I shower' or 'burning skin after water contact', and for many years I found nothing. Yet on this random day in 2015, my search flagged an article that would go on to change my life. It was a young lady in America, with almost identical symptoms to me, who had shared her diagnosis with a local newspaper. I printed the article, booked an appointment with my doctor for the following day and took a deep breath. I was seventeen at this point and had given up on the idea that my symptoms were being caused by anything but my mind. I had been medically gaslit, and I felt robbed.

It was only a few months after I printed that article, that I found myself sat in St Thomas' Hospital in London, where I was diagnosed with a skin condition called aquagenic pruritus. As I had suspected for a long time, I was having water-induced allergic reactions on my skin. I had fantasised about the day I *finally* got my diagnosis since childhood, so I expected that day to bring a sense of relief. The relief did come, but it passed quickly. I felt *angry*. As the months passed, I learnt more about my diagnosis and what it meant for me as a young person. I learnt that my condition would likely worsen with age, it was rare, hard to treat and almost impossible to pinpoint the cause. I quickly realised that my only options were *pain* or *avoidance*. I could choose to bathe, shower, wash my hair, go outside on a rainy day and accept the pain, or I could avoid those things. Avoidance sounds nice, but it isn't sustainable, because eventually . . . you're going to need a bath, or you'll be caught in the rain.

It feels like I mentally blacked out after my diagnosis, because the grieving process was so intense. I was grieving the childhood I lost to doctors' appointments. I was grieving the future I had envisioned for myself as an able-bodied person. I was grieving the fact that I had believed I had lost my mind. I ran on autopilot through the next six years of doctors' visits, investigations into my condition and courses of treatment. I quickly lost close contact with my friends, because I couldn't think about anything but my diagnosis and the time it took to get there. While my friends were making weekend plans for nightclubs and summertime festivals, I was getting excited to hear back from skin specialists. Something that was meant to bring me relief had made me feel even further away from my peers and I felt more isolated than ever. After a while, I lost my job because I was spending more time on pain management than productivity. For every hour spent working, I'd spend another two hours having allergic reactions. I didn't just lose my employment, but I lost my sense of *purpose*. I went from financially supporting myself to becoming dependent on my parents again at twenty-one years old. It felt like failure.

In the following months, as I spent more time alone with myself, I began to look at myself more closely. I saw that my body – the one I had spent the last twenty-plus years getting to know – had morphed into something else entirely. I examined my skin, realising that I had never seen it look so defeated and hurt. I scrutinised the fact that the career I'd spent the past four years pursuing was gone, because I was *physically incapable*. My friends weren't around to talk to, because they were at university, working full time or partying. It felt like everything I had known had changed overnight. I was watching the domino effect of *one* medical diagnosis, but the falling dominoes were my *life*. For the next six months, I went through a grieving process like one I've never endured before. I grieved my life, my body and my diagnosis for a long time, convincing myself that there would be no room for ambition alongside my illness. I hyper-focused on getting 'better', because it felt like the only way that I wouldn't have to say goodbye to the dreams I had before my diagnosis. I told myself that if I got better, put my head down and went through all the medical treatment, then I'd be able to focus on getting back everything I had lost. I'd reunite with my friends, get my job back and slowly start making steps towards the life I had planned. I'd work hard, buy a house, get married, have children and raise them to be happy and healthy. Do you know how long I hyper-focused on getting better? *Seven years.* Nothing else mattered to me, except *getting better*. Then, everything would be okay.

As I approached my seventh year of medical treatment for aquagenic pruritus, I realised that we were quickly running out of treatment options. Everything I had tried during those seven years had made my symptoms less tolerable, which led the NHS to explain to me that I would most likely live with aquagenic pruritus forever. They said the only thing they could focus on would be making my pain 'manageable', instead of aiming for me to 'get better'. I began a private medical journey in 2021, seeking medical care in Germany for my condition. My condition was steadily worsening, with my symptoms beginning to show signs of allergic reaction *inside* my body. When I handed my medical care over to doctors in Germany, the concern they showed towards my suffering was like nothing I had ever experienced before. The doctor mentioned potential causes of my condition could be a rare blood cancer, hepatitis B or something even more serious, which was why they suspected my treatment for aquagenic pruritus had been unsuccessful. If the NHS had been treating the wrong cause, there's no wonder we hadn't seen positive results. The NHS refused to investigate my condition further and are content with my diagnosis of aquagenic pruritus, confident they've done the most they can do to treat my symptoms.

The NHS giving up on my treatment changed *everything*.

I had spent seven years in isolation, hoping I'd reach a level of wellness allowing me to be able to resume my life as if nothing had happened. I felt that I would be doing my friends an injustice to show up as 'Niah with the water allergy', because it wasn't the version of 'Niah' they had befriended years prior. I felt that in order to deserve my friends or pre-diagnosis life back, I needed to be well and show up as pre-diagnosis Niah. Do you want the truth? I don't know that Niah any more. I had spent so much time seeing myself as 'broken' because of my illness, but it *actually* shaped me. Before my diagnosis, I wasn't aware of the things I could overcome with the power of my mind. I didn't realise that being a young, disabled person isn't mutually exclusive with losing yourself. When your body becomes less physically capable, your mind begins to compensate for it. Now, instead of hyper-focusing on 'getting better', I hyper-focus on what will fill me with accomplishment, joy and appreciation for myself.

As my medical care is now privately funded, I am faced with the task of fundraising to continue trying to investigate and treat my worsening symptoms. I don't know if I'll ever 'get better', but I won a better prize than wellness. I get to teach other young people that your diagnosis will send you into a state of grief, but you *can* make it out with your soul still alive. The day I realised that I'm not getting better was one of the best days of my life, because it enabled me to see that my diagnosis doesn't limit me. I can accept myself in any form, with any condition and still know exactly who I am and why this world needs me. I'm now twenty-five years old, with the knowledge that it takes some people a lifetime to reach the levels of acceptance I have. I am blessed, I am grateful, and I am the epitome of resilience.

Close To Quitting

LARRY LAMB

Actor

I was blessed from boyhood with an abundance of physical strength; if it had been matched with an equal amount of mental ability l might well have become a rocket scientist. However, nobody made me aware of the fact that you're only going to get one body in this life and that you'd be very well advised to look after it and not take for granted a gift like I'd been given.

Throughout my childhood and on through my teenage years I always worked; in my father's fish and chip shop from about seven years old onwards, often hauling sacks of potatoes that actually outweighed me, and then as I got older working on a stall on the local market, where I shifted tons of fruit and vegetables every week. I remember the response of a doctor at seeing the first scan of my lower back I'd ever had; he asked me if I'd started lifting heavy weights when I was very young, as it was all there to see on the screen.

Not that I misused it intentionally; I always kept myself fit and exercised regularly. The problem was that I recognised no limits to what I could lift, pull, push or carry, which is fair enough when you're young, but once you get into your middle years it's better to recognise that you do have limitations. I did exactly the opposite at precisely that period of my life, when I got involved in rebuilding an old house, which for me meant actually doing a lot of the heavy work myself. I would get people in to do the skilled part of whatever the current stage of the job involved, while I provided the muscle.

The project and the things that sprang up from it carried on for over twenty years and, while I gained a great deal of practical knowledge by watching experts do things, I was wearing my poor old body out. There were plenty of warning signals, primarily lower back pain that culminated in nerve damage, but I managed to keep it all under control with regular exercises and a lot of walking, running and swimming. But damage was still being done that I had no way of measuring, or actually being really aware of; over the course of my sixties, I always felt that I was pretty indestructible and would carry on forever.

Then I hit my seventies and things started to go wrong that weren't so easy to put right with exercise. My body was trying to tell me something but I was so determined to be completely in charge, I carried on with my life the same as ever. Early into my seventy-first year I had a big shock. On my regular Sunday morning walk my legs literally conked out and I had to force them to carry me back home; then shortly after that, I started to get a lot of strange electrical shocks running across my back, shoulder to shoulder.

A scan of my whole spine showed that years of misuse had resulted in my lower back being a terrible mess; but that wasn't what was causing all the very alarming symptoms with my legs and shoulders. The neurologist who'd organised the scan showed me where the problem was, all the way at the top of my spine; one of my uppermost discs had been so damaged it was coming very close to severing my spinal cord.

I was sent home to lie flat on my back and wait to be operated on. As I lay there with my body performing all sorts of really alarming contortions that I had absolutely no control over, it became more and more clear that, while I'd been very lucky, the problem had been pinpointed and something was going to be done about it, this whole mess was all of my own doing. The operation was a huge success; the damaged disc was removed and replaced with a composite one and the vertebrae above and below it caged together, so that my spine was effectively back in working order. That was the good news; the bad news has taken almost three years to present itself to me on a day-by-day basis.

Contrary to what I'd hoped, the jammed-up spinal cord didn't just go back to its old state, allowing the messages to travel the way they were designed to do; nerve damage can repair itself but it is painfully slow and with the accent on painfully. Over the course of the thirty-one months since the operation, every minute of every day has been a battle to get my body working properly. I was told by a highly respected physiotherapist that most men of my age when confronted with the situation I found myself in after the operation just gave up and reverted to at best walking sticks or more likely a wheelchair. That was not going to be the way for me; I'd got myself into this mess and I would do my utmost to get myself out of it.

The neurologist had spotted the problem and the surgeon had sorted it out and repaired my body; so now, as the one responsible for everything that had happened, I had to play my part. Never once in my life did I think I would ever be in such a situation but, as despondent and depressed as it has at times made me, I am determined to get myself back in shape. I will never give up.

My Thoughts Do Not Need To Become My Actions
KEVIN HINES

Storyteller

He is ancient yet ageless
He is ticking yet timeless
He runs not hunted he chases
He is a man of many faces
He is the darkness, I am the light
I may be cracked, I will never be broken

This is the bipolar mind.

I never wanted to quit, I believed that I had to! I believed I had no other course of action. It was not a decision to die by my hands; instead, I was compelled to die by suicide. Since my survived attempt, I have dedicated my existence to suicide prevention, brain health and mental wellbeing. 99.9 per cent of the people who have done what I did have passed on. None of them in the last near-century get to share their stories. I lived. I get to be here. My level of gratitude for this life knows no bounds.

I truly appreciate every single millisecond I walk this Earth. I am grateful for every place I get to go, because I didn't build those places, yet I get to experience them. I appreciate every thing I get to do because it almost didn't happen, and I am so very grateful for every person I get to meet one day at a time. As they come they are my greatest gift next to my faith in God.

Although I won't push that onto anyone else, my faith and prayers keep me grounded, hopeful, and help me remain filled with love and light and an immense capacity for joy.

Struggling daily with my brain health is normal now, I accept it, but I have the tools and techniques to alter my mood when I am depressed. I have mastered the effort to remove myself from an anxiety or panic attack through education, research and understanding. When I fly into a manic euphoric natural high and find myself filled with grandiosity, I know how to bring myself back to ground. When I have hallucinations, auditory and visual, I know how to delineate between the false reality and our true reality. That took over twenty years to conquer.

Every waking moment past the day I should have died has led me to find a reason to stay. Every single day. Day by day, step by step, and they're all baby steps; I will forever remain until I die of natural causes. I will never try to 'quit' again. I will always #beheretomorrow

Life Without Love
ANONYMOUS

It's Eid, it's my eighth birthday and my cousin is getting
married; she's nineteen and is marrying her high school
sweetheart. She's having her nikkah (Islamic wedding) at her
in-laws' and everyone is happy. Soon afterwards, people start
saying, 'When are you getting married?' But my eight-year-old
self can really see the happiness and the love. Her mum and
dad are beaming with pride.

My uncle says she needs to give up the football boots first.
My mum interjects and says her daughter will find a husband
who accepts her. She's a child. Let her enjoy herself, her time
will come and I can't wait till she finds an honourable husband.

Although raised Muslim, I never felt the pressure to be
married or get married. But I always knew the importance of it
in my culture. I would always hear 'the day you get married is
the day you complete half your deen'. So 50 per cent of my
whole purpose on this Earth is to get married and that will be
pleasing to my Lord and my family. Fast forward, I lost my
mother at an early age and around that time I have a hole in
my heart.

I can't ever remember having a crush on boys. When
playing kiss chase in the playground I used to run for my life!
But I remember the first time I got a tingling sensation and
when I felt warm. I started crushing on my female teachers
and then my female peers.

The bonds that I built with my friends growing up only got stronger and I found myself one of the only girls amongst boys. I had exactly the same interests.

I'm at uni and my first romantic interaction with a woman was in a club in Cambridge, I was far from home. Hardly knew anyone; although my friends were English I still felt very judged and taboo. There was no one like me. So, me being me, I'd talk to girls in the disguise that I was wingmanning for the boys. This one interaction got so intense I ended up kissing the girl.

I'd never been so turned on in my life. I continued to explore and had every app under the sun.

Years went past and I was dressing more and more like a stud, I'd developed toxic masculine traits and would date multiple women at the same time.

I just couldn't figure out why I wasn't falling in love and they were, so quickly.

I met this one girl, different to everyone I'd dated. Something was so endearing. I realised a lot of the women I was dating had motherly traits, as in they would cook, clean, be nurturing, overly smothering. I had to ask myself, am I looking for a girlfriend or a mum?!

This girl did none of that. Although feminine in terms of looks, she was very much career-driven; nurturing did not come naturally to her and during my relationship I unlearnt all of the toxic traits. I found acceptance that no woman will ever fill that role in my life, that no woman will love me unconditionally like my late mother, and it's fair to say I found peace with that.

I tapped into my feminine energy, learnt how to cook, do my own laundry and be the caregiver in the relationship. I found this brought me closer to my mum, acting in service and making people around me feel good.

I still wasn't happy. As I get older more and more of my friends and family are getting married, and as I'm approaching forty I'm realising, as much as I've found myself, I lost God.

I prayed for the first time in years, and I couldn't help but feel this guilt. It wasn't guilt that I was carrying because of 'my sins' but guilt in a sense where I've been so distant from God.

As I read and learnt about my religion I came to the conclusion that being who I am will not take me out of the fold of Islam – the same way if anyone committed a major sin then Allah may forgive them. I found peace with that.

But I'd had sex outside of marriage and on top of that with the same sex. Irrespective of whether heterosexual or not it's still a sin. For years I tried to justify a way where I could have both. But I can't. So I have to choose. I can't rewrite holy scripture.

But what I can do is find peace with it.

They say God puts the biggest tests on the one he loves the most.

So I have to appreciate the level of love God must have for me. Taking my mother so young and me having these inclinations. So do I accept a life without a loved one? Do I force myself to marry someone I'm not sexually attracted to?

For these questions I still don't have an answer, but what I will say is that without marriage, without children, without parents, there is still love. The love of my Lord. And I feel his love every single day.

I write this entry not to persuade you to do the same or the opposite. But to allow diversity of thought and narrative when it comes to lgbtq+. To think that we all share the same voice, have the same opinion, is not inclusive at all.

Perspective

DAN DARE

Songwriter and producer

Searching in and under the car as my mum arrived empty-handed from the hospital without my newborn brother. He had died at birth. That made my mum lose her mind. I remember as a kid her asking women on our street with pushchairs, 'Have you got my baby in there?' Skip forward twelve years, I then had two younger sisters but my mum was still suffering. She told me one night she packed my sisters in the car and drove to a cliff to drive off the side. I remember thinking that's so selfish. Until I got to that point myself, at my darkest hour standing on a train platform weeping, waiting for the train to come so I could jump in front of it, only to bump into the man in front of me as he turned round shocked. I was so possessed by the obsession of taking my own life and taking the fast route to ease my pain that I didn't even see him in front of me. Suicide isn't selfish, it's the final symptom of depression, it's the outcome of carrying the weight by yourself and not speaking about how you feel.

I had everything society told me I should have as a grown up: a house, a career, I had just signed a publishing deal and moved into a studio in Chelsea – which I had been working towards my whole life.

I hadn't dealt with the abuse or spoken about the things that weighed me down from a young age, losing my brother and the pain I saw my mother in being two of them, but also being actively in a toxic long-term relationship when I didn't have the tools to communicate or express myself so everything was magnified by 100.

The next day I met a friend for a twenty-minute chat in a cafe that changed my life. Everything became a bit lighter and manageable.

I was twenty-five.

I've since then taken back the power and made myself the observer of my thoughts, controlling the imp in my mind with exercise, therapy, mindfulness and meditation.

I'm still not 100 per cent happy despite all the successes and achievements personally; money plus material things don't matter when you finally get them. I would trade riches and success for internal peace and happiness any day of the week, but I realise it's a marathon not a sprint and I will get there in the end.

Through Your Beauty, Through Our Grief
HUSSAIN MANAWER

Through all I loved you
I pay with tears
Through all my luck too
I hold our years
I eternally internally trust you
You still, ripped me there
I feel, I sense, I must do,
Somewhere near that your close by here

Through the nights I can't sleep
Through the sound of your voice I feel, but you not speak
Through every missing piece of my peace
I find I search the little of you I keep
Through your beauty I stand
Through our loss - I fight through our grief

Through true love, I am able
To trust your angels,
To ensure our stable
Will never lose the rhythm to the rock of our cradle

Through our grief that's intertwined
Combined with a loss that's designed divine

Wishfully hoping my words will keep us alive
As I was never prepared to say goodbye

Through the nights I can't sleep
Through the sound of your voice I feel, but you not speak
Through every missing piece of my peace
I find I search the little of you I keep
Through your beauty I stand
Through our loss
I fight through our grief

I Need You To Fly

SONNA RELE AND HUSSAIN MANAWER

Singer-songwriter, artist and soul tie

I need you to fly high
Don't ever lose your will to be able to fly – high
Go straight over the hills
Don't be afraid
You need to be fearless
Need to be brave
Don't lose your focus
I need you fly – high,
Over the clouds

I was 14 when I had a moustache
15 I hit the unibrow
18 coming home and the traditions of culture are asking me if
I'm ready to go uni now

And It was around 21 I reckon
Where anxiety wasn't a question
And I can't even love myself
That's what happens when you tap out to depression

Then you get the summers full of weddings
And everyone wants to know

When you're getting married
Or if you're still moving on the low

But when it's community vs culture
Just because of respect to the elders
My generation . . .
There're still certain things we don't show

I need you to fly high
Don't ever lose your will to be able to fly – high
Go straight over the hills
Don't be afraid
You need to be fearless
Need to be brave
Don't lose your focus
I need you fly – high,
Over the clouds

You see, I was 26 and broke when Mum died
Lost faith when hope lied
Had a crisis at the midlife there's no lie
But that was a message telling me to fly because life was
moving on time

I rode sentence, I done time
In my mental doing Mum time
And realised when life took me across the border
It hit a bit harder when the poet hasn't even wrote a punch line

Now every day, it's just deep vibes,
With more deep vibes
Life threw me in a tank

Thought I wasn't going to sea life
There aint no peers
This aint the seaside
My boys are saying we're glad you came,
Finally a voice like mine is coming out of the East side

Now there calling us a bunch of animals
But what did you expect?
When the boy had a wildlife

That's why, over the clouds,
I need you to fly

I need you to fly high
Don't ever lose your will to be able to fly – high
Go straight over the hills
Don't be afraid
You need to be fearless
Need to be brave
Don't lose your focus
I need you fly – high, over the clouds

Us Two Fight Every Day
SURFING SOFAS

Poet and writer

I felt like a stack of quiz magazines,
a pile of problems and issues.
I'm sure I've shed enough tears
to go through boxes of tissues.
Ashamed of what I got into,
I had my confidence stripped too.
You want to quit and I relate,
because I wanted to quit too.

Some want me to open up,
cos I stay closed and nothing less.
Hard to bench press the stress,
so hold it on my chest.
I've been a broken little mess,
homeless and depressed.
Driven to insanity, I guess
my chauffeur's not the best.

There's been times that became
too dark to see the light.
Never knew what to do,
and it was hard to even write,
and hard to sleep at night.
Needed the nightmares to die,

so I can bring my remaining
shards of dreams to life.
Earlier I said that I wanted to quit too,
but the truth is,
that every single day,
I find I fight with quitting.
My eyes are black, my lip is split,
and teeth of mine I find are missing.
Cos every single day, I'm fighting quitting,
and at times, it's like it's winning.

At times, it truly angers me,
how some are dealt a bad hand
and expected to play
this game of life, enthusiastically.
But the cards that I've been dealt,
are what I'm working with.
I've played this game of life for years,
and what I've learned, is this . . .

They'll be times where we lose,
but we can replay the missions.
And our XP will level up
as we gain our wisdom.
If they try not to hear us,
then we'll make them listen.
and turn tables,
kinda like a DJ's equipment.

Whenever life wants to challenge you
and give you a test,
the only thing that I want you to

give is your best.
It's time to give it your best,
until every negative voice
that lives in your head,
decides to give it a rest.

Keep giving your force.
Keep giving your best.
Keep giving them more,
and cease giving them less.
Keep giving your all.
Keep giving your love.
The only thing I don't want you
to be giving . . . is up.

PART TWO

Hustle

NICK JONES
HUSSAIN MANAWER
AJ WAVY
ARNAS FEDARAVIČIUS
JAKE WOOD
CORIN HARDY
CORINNA BROWN
MICHEAL WARD
GLEN POWELL
MURRAY CUMMINGS
MICHAEL ADEX
JAY ELLIS
DANNY RAMIREZ
MARYAM PASHA
ANONYMOUS
KIRAN SONIA SAWAR
MARO ITOJE
TYLER WEST
COLIN SALMON

Never Be Afraid Of Not Succeeding – A Conversation
NICK JONES

Founder of Soho House and friend

NICK: Along the journey there've been many many pitfalls, walls and reasons not to do something. Lots of reasons why something wasn't possible, life is full of obstacles. I suppose one of the things I really enjoyed at work was trying to figure out how to get around the obstacles and how to persuade people to make things happen.

HUSSAIN: How do you think you managed to get your brain to do that?

NICK: I mean, I wake up every morning positive, I do feel things. This is for everyone, things are possible to do, whenever someone says you can't do that, that's not possible, you can't get planning permission or you'll never get members, it will never work in this country, that seems a ridiculous idea, those are the words I needed to hear to make me even more determined.

HUSSAIN: Wow, you found hope in hearing no?

NICK: In a way, hope in them saying this is impossible. I think there is a standard in work where this is impossible, you will never get that, you'll never raise the money, or you'll never get that open. If you have hope there is a chance that things can happen.

HUSSAIN: Were you always like that? Or is this something that developed over time?

NICK: Well, I'm dyslexic, you're slightly differently wired and I suppose you're wired in a way that you can see things and obstacles and how to get around them in a simple way.

HUSSAIN: That's powerful; for me, when I see a problem I get overwhelmed. But only now, similar to what you are saying, I am starting to look at problems in a good light.

NICK: Yeah, and also never be frightened of the fact that you might not be able to overcome the obstacle. Take it as a learning lesson and think, 'How else can I do this?' Never be frightened of not succeeding. Because if you are frightened of not succeeding then that is something that will put you off from trying to succeed.

HUSSAIN: That's a really profound line. I think that's the name of this piece: 'Never be frightened of not succeeding'.

NICK: Yeah, never, it's a lesson. Not succeeding is just a journey, it's all about the journey.

HUSSAIN: How have you found managing your sleep with your ambition, because you are very ambitious and you have very big dreams. For me, I get too excited, then I get overwhelmed, then I can't sleep and then all I end up doing is sleeping and end up in a state of constantly napping.

NICK LAUGHS
Yeah.

HUSSAIN: As opposed to actually getting on with what I should be getting on with . . . does this make sense?

NICK: Yeah, if you don't sleep at the right time, that makes you not sleep even more. Somehow you have to park it, if you need a nap, have a nap, and there will be some nights you lie awake worried, concerned or excited – but go with it. If you go with it and don't worry about the lack of sleep, you'll end up going to sleep.

HUSSAIN: That's so interesting, and on the journey of professional success one thing I really admire about you is that you have built a family. And I think I constantly make excuses for time in not being able to fulfil a personal life alongside my professional life. We've spoken about this, how have you managed to do that?

NICK: I've been very lucky, by having a very incredible woman in my life, Kirsty, and I've always been determined when having children that I wanted them to get along with each other. I think having a sibling is a real gift, I sometimes feel in my childhood my siblings and I didn't realise how lucky we were. And they keep me grounded, sane, happy, it's nice, it's really nice.

HUSSAIN: You can tell, even when you speak about your family there's a warmth that comes from your voice.

NICK: Yeah, I know running a business, naturally I'm a pleaser, because I went into hospitality, if you go into hospitality and you like confrontation then it's probably not the industry to go into. Hospitality is about making people happy, laugh, have fun and a good time. So naturally that's where I come from. Then having to run a business and make tough decisions, be demanding of people, you know I think I had to act that out. So when I was at home, I wasn't doing the acting, I was just being myself. You can switch them around.

HUSSAIN: That's interesting, learning to switch them around. Even from speaking with you now, I think it's the perfect way to start the 'Hustle' part of the book. Because your hustle and drive is really special.

NICK: And also the hustle is never money orientated, it was never I wanted to make money, I wanted to create space for people to enjoy, have fun and meet people. I was determined to do that. Naturally there were obstacles in the way. I found it a challenge to get around them, over them or get under them.

HUSSAIN: What part of your job do you think has been the most satisfying?

NICK: Oh, seeing people happy . . .

HUSSAIN: Yeah.

NICK: Yeah, seeing people walk into a space, enjoy it, and meet people relaxed. Now I love seeing people who don't have the opportunity, to give them the opportunity to flourish.

HUSSAIN: That's beautiful. Lastly what has been your biggest lesson or blessing when it comes to global/international business?

NICK: Well, I suppose I learn a lesson every day, growing a business globally you know, every continent and every city thankfully is different. There's different ways of doing things, it would be boring if it was all the same. But, you know, people globally want to have a nice time. That's not just a one-country requirement, it's a universal thing that people want to do, laugh, have fun, relax with friends and meet new people.

The difference is people might slightly do it a different way in different countries, but fundamentally people love food, drink, nice space wherever you are in the world. So what you have to learn is all the different ways all the different countries go around making this happen, and what the rules and regulations are to make this happen.

HUSSAIN: Well, I'm glad it's you doing this, not me!

NICK LAUGHS
Okay . . .

HUSSAIN: I feel like I see you in a different light every time we speak these days, so thank you for that also!

NICK: When are you flying to America?

HUSSAIN: Monday.

NICK: Well if there's anything you need when you are out there let me know, keep in contact, and if there's anything else you need for this book, give me a ring. I'm always available.

HUSSAIN: Thank you very much, I'm going to turn my recorder off now . . .

I Got Work Tomorrow

HUSSAIN MANAWER

Nah bro I can't come out tonight man
I got work in the morning, its long i'm doing a double shift
I'm glad the conversation ended there
To be honest, I'm happy, it never expanded

The truth of the matter is
I can't afford to go out
The cost of living is affecting my life in every aspect
Impacting my mind, the way I exhale when I breath
I must be annoying the angels on my shoulders the way i lean
up against them tossing and turning when I can't sleep
And then I fall into an online hole
Angry against the world for its double standards

Is it a victim mentality to feel like I've been abandoned?
The poorest i've ever been financially
Pretty wild to believe, It's the wealthiest i've ever been mentally
Feels like i'm an overdrawn emotionally intelligent mess who's
graduated from Yale, Harvard, Oxford or Stanford

I got work in the morning,
It's better for me to do that, and not to be like people around me,
You should see what the can-did, and that's me being candid

I have to wear cheap black shoes, my feet are hurting
But these podcasts and audiobooks have got my thinking expanding
On my break I slip back quick, i revert childlike with, bad habits
For some reason I'm always comparing my life to those online,
Things I never truly even be wanting or understanding

For me this is just a job,
Really not surprised i never made it to become the supervisor
When mentally i'm so detached in my head
On the way to work
On the shop floor
On the way home
I'm an actor,
An artist,
Author, poet,
Deep sea scuba diver

And if I get the chance I volunteer to work on sets for my
dream
Get a glance, a moment of art and heart for a credit
I'd never really tell anybody my financial situation,
I wouldn't really feel comfortable,
But between me and you, I'm losing my hair and getting a lot
of white hair
Because of all these direct debits

I got work tomorrow,
It's annoying they're scrapping the overtime,
The pound i gotta stretch it
I've done a lot of healing lately
These issues im not running away from,

I'm not gonna leg it
I'll do it, i'll get it,
Positive thinking they're calling it, manifesting,
Yeah I said it,
Ah wait, stop it, forget it,

No don't, your just brave enough to speak about it,
We all get it

Each of us, is dancing with demons on the dancefloor
And the choice of music, the DJ's playing, is really making this
hardcore
That's why, we revert to our safe spaces
Next to our incense sticks, piano keys, star signs and guitar
chords

Working class, I'm really not sure if it's true what they say,
Even though I remember reading it in sociology
That we want our gratification immediately
It doesn't help that our passion can be misconstrued so
inconveniently
And we're branded as individuals that are so quick to behave
disobediently
But look seriously, don't roll your eyes at me so tediously,
We're living through challenging times,
We haven't seen times like these in previous scenes

I can't come out tonight
I got work in the morning, i'm doing a double shift
I'm glad the conversation ended there
To be honest, happy, it never expanded

The truth of the matter is
I can't afford to go out
The cost of living is affecting my life in every aspect

1-0-8-6-1-7

AJ WAVY

Son, brother, artist

1-0-8-6-1-7

The final clock-out, and it felt like heaven.

I'd known those digits for so many years,
The same routine job, the same one gear,

But pressing those buttons for one last time,
Meant a brand new beginning and a brand new climb.

So now I walk past casually, almost magically I've found myself
    waking up to a whole different reality.
From shop floors to red carpets, I take pride in the fact that this
    didn't happen randomly.
Success happens gradually.
To a focused mind and a devoted heart success happens oh so
    naturally.
I know what I'm about to say may hurt but pls try not to be
    mad at me.

Sometimes you have to give up.
Your comfort, your stability should not stand in the way of
    your true capability.

I'm not telling you to leave your job or sell your house, cos at
    the end of the day, your dreams don't always work out.
All I'm saying is every morning I get to eat my toast,
knowing the chances I took allow me to wake up and do what I
    love the most.
I get to watch my dad smile at my silly videos, even though
    some of them make him roll his eyes, he'll still wish me luck
    before every single one of my shows

A lot of people tell me giving up is wrong,
But here's the thing – giving up the right things at the right
    time is the only reason I've finally got to where I belong.

So whether you want to quit or whether you want to stay,
The choice is one that's yours to make.

Look Up

ARNAS FEDARAVIĆIUS

Actor and friend

I was twenty-four at the time. I was standing on the corner of Tottenham Court Road tube station. It was around 5 p.m. and most people had finished work so it was packed. Nobody wants to stop and talk to a stranger at this time of day, especially if that stranger is trying to hand you a leaflet selling you a discount on an app you probably don't need, or a free day at a gym, so you could get a six-month membership afterwards. That was exactly what I was doing. I smiled doing it, but inside I was sobbing. Don't get me wrong, it's a job like any other and someone has to do it. But as soon as I would notice a familiar face from my childhood coming towards me, wearing a suit, looking and being successful – I'd turn away and hide my face. I felt ashamed.

My ego must've been at an all-time high. 'I was the one who left my hometown with dreams of success, I was the one who was working on something big just a few years back, I deserve better, I do not want this job!' Those were the thoughts racing through my silly mind. The reality was a lot different – I was living in a space slightly bigger than a storage room that was meant for a cat to live in, and I haven't done any acting in a long time. Perhaps those voices from the past that said I'm aiming too high, that I am naive and that it's impossible to achieve what I set out to, were right.

I mean I am standing on a street corner with actual tears on my face and the only 'acting' I'm doing is pretending I'm fine.

Days went on in a similar fashion. A week later I just became numb to it all. Then I started quietly praying, asking for an explanation that I thought I deserved. And finally in a few weeks time I looked up and said, 'I get it.' I felt grateful for all the little things I had: I was healthy, I had food, I had an actual roof over my head, and even if they seemed far away – I had dreams. And no one would ever take them away from me. I started showing up early, even looking forward to those shifts. They became my stage to practise, perform, to sing, dance and engage with people. I don't have formal education but the time I spent being a street promoter taught me that every experience we have teaches us something about ourselves, but most importantly I learnt that whatever you do, you have got to own it.

Never half-ass it. No matter how small you think the job is – either do your absolute best or quit doing it altogether.

A few months later I got the biggest job I ever got, but I still did those shifts.

I needed to.

In case my fragile ego would ever take these gifts for granted again.

Never Quit On A Dream

JAKE WOOD

Father, husband, actor, friend

At the age of ten I began drama classes at the Anna Scher Children's Theatre, in Islington where I grew up. There was an open door policy and my mum had enrolled me because I had done some acting at primary school and enjoyed it. Attendance was twice a week after school. After three months I got a role in one episode of the police drama, *The Gentle Touch*, my first professional job as an actor. I loved the experience and decided then that this was the job I would love to pursue.

For the next twenty years I worked with moderate success as a jobbing actor. When work was scarce I worked as a painter and decorator or in telesales to supplement my income. At one point I began the Knowledge to become a black cab driver. By the age of thirty I was married, with a mortgage and thinking about starting a family. It was getting tougher and tougher, both mentally and financially, to keep going between jobs and I was disillusioned and disheartened. It became easy to look back on my professional life and at how it had all started with negative feelings . . . that I had simply stumbled into acting, I had been lucky to get that first paid job, and now I wasn't even sure if acting was what I wanted to do any more. I had lost all enthusiasm and I was questioning my own capabilities. I was at a crossroads. I had many soul-searching conversations with my wife, Alison, who always encouraged me to continue, to stay positive. To this day she remembers me very nearly walking away.

Eventually I made the decision that if I was to continue acting I had to retrain. I felt I needed a different perspective. It was my final effort to make things work. I found a drama teacher in London called Scott Williams and I signed up for his drama classes for the coming year. The method he taught was nothing like I had ever experienced before and at first I wasn't sure if it was working for me. But Scott asked me to trust him and so I committed wholeheartedly during classes. And I'm so glad that I did. Over that year I learnt so much. How to be spontaneous, how to live truthfully in each and every moment and most importantly how having a solid technique that I could rely upon gave me new enthusiasm, fresh energy and a rediscovered love for acting. Everything changed. With this experience fuelling me, I immediately landed good parts in two movies back to back and, following these, a year after finishing the course with Scott, I auditioned for and was offered the role of Max Branning in *EastEnders*, a life-changing role that I would go on to play for the next fifteen years.

I came very close to quitting on my dream. The only thing that prevented me from doing so was the openness to see things from a different point of view, the willingness to take the risk of trying something different that was out of my comfort zone and the effort of learning new skills.

On The Wings Of A Butterfly

CORIN HARDY

Director, writer and producer

My story comes from a time when a younger me embarked on
a journey to create a film that I hoped would 'put me on the
map' and become a way to make a start in the industry of film
that I had always dreamed of being a part of, but never really
knew how to make that first step.

After finishing my degree at Wimbledon School Of Art and
literally on the final day of the degree show, while packing up
my room, my equipment, my sculpting tools and camera
equipment, I was about to head off in search of a career as a
special effects makeup artist and sculptor when my tutor
Valerie Charleton collared me on the way out of the building
and asked me what I was going to do next. When I replied
about finding work at a workshop in Pinewood or Shepperton,
she looked me in the eyes and said, 'You should go and make
your own films,' and, although this was a brief encounter, it
was incredibly meaningful and changed my trajectory going
forwards.

So I wrote a short film called *Butterfly* about a boy dealing
with grief and trying to find a way out of it. I didn't have any
money and I wanted it to be epic and demonstrate my love of
visual storytelling and feel epic, so, inspired by a combination
of Ray Harryhausen's animated monster movies, Tim Burton's
The Nightmare Before Christmas and Aardman Animation's
claymation, I decided to make it using old school stop-motion

animation and embarked on my own production, which I hoped would take between two and two and a half years. I raised a small Arts Council grant and also a M.I.N.D. grant as the film deals with mental health issues. After finalising the script, storyboarding it out, I started to design the sets and the puppet characters, and while largely working alone, I called upon the help of friends, relatives and students at my old college to help create what I needed to start animating.

This part of the process alone, the making, took around two years, before I started actually animating, frame by frame. This was all done on an old 16mm wind-up Bolex camera that I bought. Using poster sticks and measuring devices, my camera rigs were built from car jacks mounted on old shower curtain rails and I loaned lighting equipment and set up a studio in my parents' old dusty wood workshop. I realised it was a huge undertaking, though I remained inspired as the days, weeks, months and years passed by, by creating things that I enjoyed – hand-crafted and made organically. No computers were involved. I had to stop for weeks at a time to raise money to live, by doing private commissioned sculptures and design work for record labels and bands – putting my art skills to use.

When I started actually animating, one frame at a time, twenty-four moves per second, it was a lonely process, spent listening to music day upon day and focusing incredibly intently on the mission at hand. To complete the movie.

Seasons came and went; blisteringly hot in summer, shut in in the darkness of my studio with fans on to cool the room that was illuminated by fifty miniature lights and to stop the detailed sets and poised puppets from heat warping, and then ice-cold chilly fingers in winter, doing the same thing but with heaters on and breath in the air. Friends at the pub asked me, 'How did that little cartoon thing you were doing turn out?'

– and I answered excitedly that I was still doing it! By Year Three I had animated six minutes! They couldn't really compute this and maybe it was insane. It certainly took its toll, but I managed to remain constantly inspired by creation and seeing the magic results, bringing this puppet, this world to life. My long-term relationship fell by the wayside as I continued to animate through another year and people moved on, people died. I got older, but not really – my life felt like it was on hold, one frame at a time. Twenty-four moves per second. Repeat. I just had to complete it.

But who would know if I didn't? This was before YouTube and social media – in fact I was struck one day, approximately four years into making the film, with daunted feelings of hopelessness and a strange sense of realisation of 'What if I don't finish making this film?' And 'What if the film is shit?' And 'Would anyone even know or care?' – and when I realised that the answer was 'Not really' I had a momentary lapse of confidence and of feeling kind of worthless and it forced me to re-evaluate where I was . . .

What if all this was for nothing?

I looked at my puppets, at my beloved workspace and at the way the lights in that tiny studio made everything feel alive, and by this point I also had perhaps fourteen or so minutes of animation cut together and I could feel the film was coming together and I pushed the feeling away, because it wasn't helpful. I had come this far. For the sake of the puppets looking back up at me, for the people who had put their own time into helping me with props, costumes, equipment and advice, and for the charities that had gifted me money to make the film.

I WOULD NOT GIVE UP.

I would finish the film – no matter how long it took, it HAD to be finished. And I got back to work, one frame at a time . . .

After five years, and a lot of sound design work and recording, I completed *Butterfly*, my first official short film. It runs at around thirty minutes, it's a little crude and jerky at times, but I am still proud of it. It's pure. It's mine. And it ended up getting into a number of film festivals, beginning with Edinburgh and also Brazil, Belgium and Korea, and it caught the eye of a number of people who gave me the next break in film and music video and led to me having the career I now have as a film director, writer and producer.

So, no matter how long it takes or how hard it feels. Be resilient. And never give up.

Determination Will Keep You Growing
CORINNA BROWN

Actor and friend

Like you, I've wanted to quit too. In fact, I have quit. School subjects,
part-time jobs, hobbies and even friendships. I've quit many things
to be able to chase the dreams little me dreamed up years ago.

Quitting those things has been easy though. The ties aren't
as deep, and the care isn't there.

The dictionary definition of to quit reads: leave (a place),
usually permanently.

But in Middle English it's used in a sense of being set free.
So in these situations, that's the definition that works for me.
When it stops serving your happiness, set yourself free.
What's hard, is when it's something you love. Like I love what I
    do –
so when the thoughts start intruding,
the voice of doubt, booming . . . It's scary.

                                        imposter syndrome is real.
Even writing this now, I feel myself wanting perfection . . .
The idea (and probably reality) of not achieving that (because
    nothing and nobody is perfect) already has my brain
    singing, 'Maybe don't do it,' 'Maybe give up,' 'Oh, you've
    missed the deadline,' 'No one really gives a fu*k.'
But the fact my fingers keep typing, and the words jump down
deletes
And the words flow down
deletes

73

And the words
             hesitantly
                     creep onto the page ...
They still make their mark.
They're still heard.
And maybe that's the point.
Keep going ... even if you think your efforts aren't showing.
When it's hard and the motivation is s l o w i n g
The passion inside will always keep flowing and the
    determination will keep you **growing.**

There's Someone Higher Than Us, Looking Out For Me, Making Sure The Ship Is Getting Steered Correctly

MICHEAL WARD

Actor

'If you believe, you will achieve' are the words of my second primary school motto, John Bramston in Hainault, so simple but effective. And subconsciously that has stayed with me. I've seen it, I've felt that one line and its profound impact on me.

I was in Year 8 in Chadwell Heath High School and I took part in the Shakespeare's School Festival when I played Macduff in a *Macbeth* production. As well as playing football, it was clear I had a passion for drama. If I never had played football, I would have known this a lot earlier but I loved football and thought for a long time that football was what I was going to do because it's what I favoured most.

But when it came to football, I had to have an honest conversation with myself with regards to my ability. I always felt I was good, but honestly speaking, just not good enough. For me, to pursue something, I need to want to be the best at it. It's not enough for me to aspire. With football, I wanted to play matches, I loved the competition of it and that gave me my sensations, however with drama, I fell in love with the process of it all. I loved being able to figure things out, I loved the training of acting, whereas I didn't enjoy the training of football.

I found that I was doing drama in my own time more often and my friends were all playing sports. I did originally try to encourage them to come and even when they didn't, I still went. But there was a clear instinctive joy I got from drama that I really couldn't ignore. When I think back to John Bramston, I think of this performance we did in Year 6 for a musical called *The Wind in the Willows* – it was something I really enjoyed. I remember really wanting to be engaged with it.

I went on to pick Drama for GCSE and once high school was over, I pursued it alongside Maths, Geography and Physical Education for my A levels at sixth form. However, soon into my sixth form, I really found it wasn't for me. I began losing interest and all I really cared about was doing something more practical in Drama. There was so much coursework in sixth form along with a strict schedule. When I turned 17, I contemplated entering 'The Face of JD' modelling competition. A close friend of mine from school told me about this and prior to this my mum had spent a lot of money on a modelling portfolio for me.

My mum has always been so supportive – even throughout my football days, she was always checking in and making sure I'm good. When I first told her about 'The Face of JD', she encouraged me to do it. And after entering, eventually I became one of the winners. This was pretty mad. I remember me, my mum and my sister (who had to take the day off school) travelling up North for our first time for a shoot. We got the train to Manchester. It was fun, I was young and it was different and unexpected, especially as I was now doing a shoot for a place I shopped at.

My mum's always believed in me, no matter what I did, she supported my decisions. There were times where I could have strayed. I didn't have the money to do things and the environment we grew up in was not easy. There are so many distractions and not many fruitful things to be doing in terms of building towards something positive. And if I didn't have my mum's support guiding me down a path, things could have been different.

Having spent a year in sixth form, I found myself complaining a lot, I wasn't enjoying my time there and I began hating it. I've always been a person who says, 'whatever I'm going to do in life, I've gotta enjoy it'. I knew I wasn't enjoying this any more. I also wasn't willing for it to put me in a rut, even though it kinda almost did. The only thing I enjoyed in sixth form was the practical side of Drama but there wasn't much of it, there was so much coursework and that's another thing I couldn't stand. I knew there had to be a course out there with more practical elements.

I then went to visit Epping College and instantly noticed the split between practical and coursework was completely different to what I had been studying. I still remember being blown away by how big the theatre was, the spaces within the college, the atmosphere, everything as a whole was a lot more relaxed with fewer rules. And seeing as I was still the face of JD Sports, I could attend shoots in Manchester if I needed to also.

It was here I met a great teacher called Ellie Nelson. On my first day, she was the person showing me around the college, the spaces and she also happened to be the main Performing Arts teacher. She was really helpful. I remember her telling me, it's a musical theatre course so you have to sing and dance. I didn't really know if I could do that, so I went back to sixth form. I stayed for one more week and then went back to see Ellie at Epping College. I told her, I'm going to be joining and I remember her being super excited by that.

I then quit sixth form and began attending Epping College. Ellie left the college after a year but whilst she was there she helped me a lot and put me up for a lot of auditions. I did an audition for a drama school but it didn't go well at all. Shortly afterwards, there was an exciting opportunity for me to audition for an American pilot. Here are the scenes you need to prepare with a song, they said (in those days, I still couldn't sing so I decided to rap two songs I love merged together). The audition went well, the scenes were amazing, along with the song I let the nerves do what they needed to do and I got some amazing feedback from the casting director. I didn't get the job. They said I was quite green, which means fairly new. But the feedback was that the casting director loved me. A few days later, I went on to meet my current agent, Gavin Mills.

I didn't think it would be possible to leave college and not train and just be with an agent, but I had to trust the process. I signed with Olivia Bell Management and began trusting Gavin's vision for me. I then got a job at William Hill in Romford so I could start earning some money and whilst working I began auditioning regularly, luckily being able to learn my lines whilst at work. This job really did work in my favour.

I began noticing that acting seemed to be calling for me in my life and it was something that could lead to an incredible career path.

I went up for another role that required an American accent – I never got the job, but the feedback was the most important thing for me. Throughout the first year of being with Gavin, I got my first paid job, a music video for Tom Walker for a song called 'Blessings' (when I think about that now, it's amazing). I was doing short films and then I landed my first role in a show called *The A List*. And whilst filming *The A List*, I booked another role to play a character called Jamie Tovell in *Top Boy*.

And little did I know that playing Jamie in *Top Boy* would change my life, forever.

The pace that everything was happening throughout *Top Boy* was incredible, things were moving so fast, struggles, decisions and opportunities presented themselves. But one thing that really stands out the most is the overwhelming flow of love that was directed at me. I learned so much from working on *Top Boy*, the freedom to play with the role, expression, experience as a whole but I learned to slow down and once again trust and enjoy the process.

I remember at the *Top Boy* premiere, Drake said to me, 'Are you ready?' and I was like, 'what do you mean?' He said, 'it's going to be crazy bro,' and that's when I realised, maybe this was actually going to be bigger than I thought. You can never quite prepare yourself. Throughout filming *Top Boy*, I thought my life was going to change but you can never really know the intricacies and details of what that's really going to be like for you. I thought it was going to be young Black people that would know who I was, but the support and love has been incredible from people from all different walks of life, young, old, celebrities, literally everyone. And predominantly it is young Black people, which is special because our stories are important.

Things moved quickly for me from there. I was filming a movie in New Jersey, and the day before the *Blue Story* film premiere, my agent arranged a group call and told me I had been nominated for the EE BAFTA Rising Star Award. 'You're lying!' I responded. It didn't seem real to me when I was there, by the stage at the award show and this was all going out to the world.

I definitely feel blessed, therefore I try my best to deliver, to enjoy myself and to learn as much as I possibly can every day that I am on set, and even throughout filming *Empire of Light* I was still learning to hit my mark. I'm always learning, I'm always gaining an education from the world around me. I've also learned, if you follow that spark, believe in that spark, things can be achieved. And just so you know, that Year 11 trophy I picked up for being the class clown still holds a special place in my family home.

The Passion Of My Life

GLEN POWELL

Actor, writer, producer, son, brother, uncle, friend

In the face of failure, there was a time when I struggled to even put food on the table. There were moments when I found myself repeating, 'I don't think this is going to work out,' as I poured everything I had into my aspirations. Despite the uncertainty, I had to engage in a sort of self-deception, convincing myself that everything would eventually fall into place, even though deep down I knew there was a strong chance it would not.

To know me is to know my failures – they've been an integral part of my journey. I haven't been handed anything; every inch I've gained has been fought for. I was confronted by people telling me bluntly that this path wasn't meant for me, urging me to give up on my dreams, once and for all. I would look in the mirror and think, 'Am I crazy or is this just the gauntlet that will make this all worth it?' It wasn't a moment where I was going to quit, but it was a moment where I had to think, am I the person I think I am? Is this going to end ugly? I am putting everything I have into something and it's just not going to work out? At the end of the day, I don't believe I'm that special, I just believe I work harder than everybody else.

In Los Angeles, failure feels inevitable. A town where your worth is loud and your value to other people is palpable. You wonder if the universe is signalling you to quit or maybe it's time to refuel the car one last time, use your last dime to hit the gas, and never look back. This is the moment where the self-storytelling helps because it overpowers logic. That moment when you have to double down on yourself, and go alright, it's me versus the world. I'm just going to have to out-work everybody. And for me, that is why even after a day of failure I can look myself in the mirror. I left it all on the field.

For me, my unwavering passion for filmmaking has been my greatest asset. I've been enamoured with movies and the craft of acting for as long as I can remember. The joy I find on a film set is unparalleled; it's where I feel most alive. Every day, I wake up with a burning desire to tell stories that resonate with people, to make an impact through the powerful medium of film. It's an endless quest for education and inspiration.

My buddy who I've known for years, before anything happened, recently said to me, 'Anyone who hasn't seen you from the beginning can't truly understand what it takes . . . When people ask me, how did Glen make it out in Hollywood? I tell them he put in 18-hour days for every day as long as I have known him, he refuses to give up, he refuses to stop working, until he makes this happen.'

One of the things my parents told me when I was a kid was, 'do what you have to do, so you can do what you want to do'. There's certainly going to be failure, so you can go back home and give up or you can double down on yourself and just out-hustle everyone around you. If you want it, do what you have to do.

Don't Forget To Enjoy Yourself
MURRAY CUMMINGS

Director

I wanted to quit too.
I did quit, many many times.
But something kept asking me
Why are you stopping doing things you love?
Because you won't be the best in the world?
That's no reason to stop something.
Does it make you happy? Yes.
Do it then. Do it every day.
Enjoy yourself.
Make something, anything.
Put it out into the world.
Feel that nervous excitement.
Don't quit
Keep going.
Do it again, many many times.

Hustlers' Mentality

MICHAEL ADEX

Entrepreneur and CEO of NQ

'Hustle' is a word that for me resonates even more in today's society, with so much more opportunity but arguably less institutional help; many young people have no choice but to hustle. My journey is defined by that very word, coming from not the best area in Manchester with not so many opportunities to realise my potential; I had to hustle to create them. In the generation we are in now, we are blessed to be able to make a living through non-traditional means. Having dropped out of university at 19 to pursue a career in music, one of my passions at the time, I think it's more important now to pursue things you are passionate about to hopefully create opportunities for yourself.

1. **Passion** – The art of hustling requires having to convince people, showing them how much you believe in the things that you are saying; having passion and showing it makes people buy into you more.

2. **Discipline** – Enroute to your destination, there will always be things that get in the way or stuff you don't necessarily want to deal with. That's when you need to have discipline to keep you on track.

3. **Resilience** – Similarly to discipline, you have to be resilient

when it comes to knock backs as that's inevitable when chasing any dream.

4. **Curiosity** – They say 'curiosity killed the cat', but I believe it opens up doors that you never thought to imagine. When hustling, you're always looking for a competitive advantage – being curious can help you discover this.

5. **Conviction** – To succeed you must always hustle with conviction – attempting to hustle halfheartedly will only lead to halfhearted results.

The Importance Of The Vision – A Conversation
JAY ELLIS

Actor and dear friend

HUSSAIN: Here we are, the last time I interviewed you was for my YouTube channel Hussain's House in my garden shed around ten years ago.

JAY: It may even be more than that.

HUSSAIN: A lot has changed.

JAY: It's been a long time.

HUSSAIN: And here we are in your beautiful home in Los Angeles, and I get to watch you go from award shows to TV shows to movies to late-night talk shows, and you still find the time to be so present for everyone in your life.

JAY: I mean, I guess I really don't know any other way, people have been present in my life, so that is one thing I understand where it's gotten me to where I'm at and that is being present. And on the flip side all of this stuff is amazing, beautiful and like you're in rooms with people you'd never imagine you'd be in rooms with and it's all mind-blowing, for me it's super important to take a step back to have perspective over all of it. Also to be thankful but also realising the reason I am in the room or in those spaces a lot of it is because of the people in my life.

HUSSAIN: For as long as I have known you, you've always had a vision . . .

JAY: Yeah, I mean the vision changes over time but there are some core pieces of the vision that have always been there. I also feel that I live in this world that is so imaginative and we get to create for a living and create stories for a living that I should be able to create a vision for what I want my career and life to be. If I can create a character then I should be able to create that as well.

HUSSAIN: Wow.

JAY: For me, there always has been a vision and that's the thing I walk towards and stay focused on. But I think in times where I get distracted or stressed or thrown from one thing to another, I think that vision is the thing I always come back to as a centring point to be like this is why I am here and this is the thing I want to be doing. For me it's been a healthy check, a healthy reminder as to why I am on the path, as to why I do what I do, and why I love what I do, because if I stay focused on that I get to experience all these other things on the way.

HUSSAIN: When we first met each other all them years ago, walking through Stratford Westfield, did you have the vision then?

JAY: I think I had the vision from the moment I knew I wanted to be an actor. I don't think I never not had the vision. I think again, the vision has shifted as my knowledge and experience has changed and grown. I've learnt more and been exposed to more. It's definitely always been there. I've always known what I want.

HUSSAIN: How do you stay so calm and patient?

JAY: How do you not?

I don't know how to not stay calm and patient, I think a part of it is naturally who I am as a person. I try to stay present and stay grounded and be in the moment and take things in. Then I think the other piece is, because of that vision, not that the work is never done, but I'm on the path to the vision, I am taking the steps that I need to take. For me I always say I feel like I'm always where I'm supposed to be. For every moment, every room I'm in, every project, every award show, I am where I am supposed to be in the moment for the vision. I also think that we all have destructive behaviours but the thing I come back to if it's not serving my purpose or serving my vision I need to find a way to put it in check and not let it take me away from the things I want to do and achieve.

HUSSAIN: That's really incredible developing that . . .

JAY: It's hard, I don't think it's easy by any means, but I do I think for a while every day you have to check in with yourself and then maybe it becomes every three days and then maybe it becomes once a week, then once every two weeks, then once a month then once a quarter. But I think you constantly have to have these check-ins with yourself and these little reminders to have real conversations with yourself and be

like, 'Is this distracting? Is this destructive? Is this serving
me? Is this not serving me? What could I be doing instead of
X that could be serving my goal or my dreams?' And if I don't
know something can I put my ego aside enough to say I don't
know and I want to go learn. Because I think that's another
thing, I have got distracted before by letting my ego get in the
way and then I have to go all the way back and start over
when I could have just done it in the beginning.

HUSSAIN: So self-awareness is definitely really key.

JAY: Self-awareness is insanely key, for me, everyone is
different. Self-awareness for me is where I am in the
industry, where I am in the city, where I am in a state, in the
world. Just remembering so much life exists outside of this
room I am in right now and just being able to step back with
perspective. I think sometimes for me, it really helps me
keep self-awareness there.

HUSSAIN: Amazing, this book is called *I Wanted to Quit Too*
and it's stories from inspirational people I have met on this
journey of life. Has there ever been a moment where you felt
like quitting?

JAY: Yeah, plenty of times, I think I did quit, when I very first
started acting I quit and walked away from it for like two or
three years.

HUSSAIN: Wow, I didn't know this.

JAY: I went and got a day job, I was working retail, I did that
for a couple of years and I got laid off. My boss called me,

and she said she got laid off and said I am probably next as I'm the only person she's hired since she has been at the job, so she called me in advance to let me know to ring a headhunter and look for another job. I remember thinking to myself, I didn't move to Los Angeles to be in retail, that is not what I came here for, that's not what the vision was.

But I got distracted along the way, my ego got in the way, I got afraid of being told no and of rejection and of going through the process of getting better. And I remember thinking I never want that feeling again, I just want to go and do it, and you know hopefully it will work out. I remember finding my first acting class, trying to figure out how I was going to pay for my first class, working nights at a job, while working a job during the day just so I could go to acting class.

At one point I had three different jobs that I was rotating through around a week that would all allow me to rehearse during the daytime and then go to class at night-time a couple days a week. That's when I realised there is no going back. I did quit, I fully quit, I walked away. I was like I don't understand why I live in LA. If working in retail was what I was going to do with my life, I could live anywhere in the world and do this.

But once I got going, the rejection is hard, you have to find your way of dealing with hearing no. And for me, at a certain point I realised every no is me getting a step closer to my yes, I had to hear no. It's a numbers game to some degree. Just because this door is locked doesn't mean another door will be locked. I just had that view of what's for me will come for me when it's supposed to come for me, because I am on this path, I am on this journey and I am doing the work.

HUSSAIN: I feel like you are constantly doing the work, and being around you wants me to do more work.

JAY: Good!

HUSSAIN: For real, the last question I have for you is how do you manage your mental health?

JAY: For me there's a bunch of ways that I manage mental health. I work out a bunch, that's a big thing for me. That's a quiet time for me. It's probably the easiest time for me to compartmentalise and separate from work and just be in a space. And sometimes that can be listening to a podcast, reading a book and sometimes that can be sitting on the couch watching a TV show, but a lot of the time though I find it's in my workouts.

I also think that physically feeling good leads to mentally feeling good in a lot of ways, because you are achieving something, you are doing something and having little goals. For me, getting the big goals is about getting the little goals that you set for yourself along the way. And all those little goals add up to being the big thing that you were trying to get to, and trying to achieve. I love walking, I love going for walks, sometimes I'm on the phone talking the whole time, sometimes I'm just taking in the city. Free writing is something, every once in a while I just sit down and just write to put some words down to see what happens. And check-ins. I value sitting down with folks and saying, 'What's up, how are you doing? What's going on?' That then leads to conversation for people to ask you the same things. Being able to have those conversations knowing that you are not alone in a situation. Knowing that there's billions of us on this planet and that you are not the only person in your situation, there are of course certain situations that are very rare but we all go through a lot of similar situations and we often think we are alone so having people to speak to is huge.

HUSSAIN: I've also noticed, you have built an incredible international family. I really felt it at your wedding, I felt I knew people before I knew them!

JAY: *LAUGHS*

I got lucky, I really do believe good people find good people, I grew up with that. My family is from the South mostly and the Midwest so we are very neighbourhood people, so you know everyone. And in the last few years of my life with my work schedule being so crazy, most of my friends, even if I don't speak to them for months, we pick back up where we left off and for me that's a sign of friendship, understanding, respect and I understand my friends are hustling in their lives, doing their day jobs, with their families, and I don't fault them for that so the reciprocity of that is super important.

I'm fortunate to have people who I love, love me, love my family, and I love them and their families. And we are all very like-minded, we are goal-oriented, most of my friends have a vision board and we speak about vision boards, we speak about what we want to achieve this year and next. I really think like minds come together, not to say we all think the same, because we all challenge each other and sharpen each other, but I do think our core beliefs about friendship, love, life and how you treat people and how to be creating no matter how big or small, that will have a ripple effect that can help change people's lives for the micro or the macro. I think we all think like that, and that's from everyone in my life, from the trainer, lawyer, to other actors, make-up artists, writers, we all just want to be good people.

HUSSAIN: That's incredible, and lastly! What do you think is the biggest lesson you have learnt from all of this?

JAY: I don't know, I think I'm still learning. Every day I'm learning stuff, I think the biggest lesson I've learnt is that there is not one lesson to learn. Life is made up of so many experiences and there are so many proverbial forks in the road and just because you go down one of them doesn't mean you can't get back on your path. And just because you go down one of them and it's not what you thought it was doesn't mean there isn't something to learn from it and grow from it. And just because you go down a path that's absolutely amazing for you, means there is still something to learn and grow from it too.

The one thing I really take away from where I am at in my life, is that it's all about growth. It's all about learning and it's all about this journey that we're on that really never ends until you want it to end to some degree.

Life is meant to be lived, the good and the bad, and there is always something to take from it that will enrich you as a human, creator, mother, father, brother, sister, lover, whatever it is, there is something there we can all learn from. To me it's the alchemist's joint, it's not about the destination it's about the journey, the journey is what makes the destination sweet. It's all the stuff along the way that makes the destination sweet, if you're just focused on the destination then you're missing out on everything else along the way.

For me, that's the biggest lesson I've learnt, I'm still learning.

HUSSAIN: Amazing, thank you so much man.

JAY: Yeah man, all day bruh.

HUSSAIN: Incredible and also thanks a lot for always letting me stay!

96 – A Conversation
DANNY RAMIREZ

Actor, writer, producer, director

From the United States of America to the United Kingdom,
Danny Ramirez and Hussain Manawer jump on a
catch-up call to discuss all things hustle and healing

HUSSAIN: My man, I don't even know where to start, congratulations on everything, take me to the beginning, where did your relationship with acting come from, did you start acting in Miami?

DANNY: Thank you bro, I appreciate you, congratulations on everything to you. Even though I grew up in Miami it actually started in Atlanta where I was a freshman playing college soccer. I was an extra in a film and that inspired me to drop out of spring semester to head back to Miami to study and read on it. A few months after returning home, I had three options for the following year

1. Stay in school in Miami, live with my mom, save that money, find an acting scene close by
2. Play soccer in Missouri. If I did this I would have some extra cash in my pocket every month that I get to keep while still pursuing my soccer dreams
3. Play soccer at NYU Poly (New York University) in a big city with a more established acting community.

My mom encouraged me to make a pros and cons list for each of the places I wanted to go. I categorised it up, looking into costs, locations, acting scene, quality of life etc, tallying it up with numbers from 1–20 (20 holding the highest value).

*Example of chaotic magical system below

	Miami	New York	Missouri
Acting Scene	10	20	0
Location	19	9.5	0
Costs	9	0	18

This continued all the way down twenty categories until the last point was given. I was giving places single points or half points and then added them all up. They each equalled 96.

I couldn't believe it, I've created this chaotic point system and there's no way this could have happened. I showed my mom and her reaction was the same. She then said, *this means wherever you go, you'll be great, you'll be good, trust that.* She then told me to pick the one that was most important to me, no matter the costs.

HUSSAIN: So what did you pick?!

DANNY: I decided to go with option 2.

We're going to New York!

It's the most expensive option, but it's also the one that is directly tied with the things I want to be doing.

Even though there were many obstacles at the start I really believed this little crazy graph I made gave my mom and me confidence, because getting the same number across them is something that shouldn't happen. I'm not a big mystical numbers guy, but this felt like it meant something.

But the reality was the magical number 96 didn't take away the high price point. Although I would have access to the best teachers I could find, the sum of the student loans turned out to be $250,000. My mom really encouraged me to go and pursue my dreams. So I accepted the offer to NYU Poly.

HUSSAIN: You must have been celebrating?!

DANNY: We celebrated and I got right to work, but the celebration I remember the most was actually a weird one when I look back at it. It was midway through the semester, my mom called me when I was at the library. I could tell she was crying through the phone and she told me the loans had finally been approved. I also started crying at the library, excited but more than anything relieved I would be able to finish this semester.

What makes the celebration so weird is that someone allowed us to take a loan from them. We were celebrating that we are now in $250,000 debt, but at least I was able to participate.

HUSSAIN: What feelings overcame you?

DANNY: How much my mom put into this and that I better make something out of it. Even though the obstacles at the start were hard, I'd rather be struggling in something that I love instead of doing anything else. I had to keep reminding myself to really push through when it wasn't easy. But I had to have my mom's back just like she had mine. I had to make this work.

HUSSAIN: Did you develop or adopt different mentalities from this point?

DANNY: Yeah, this was a time in my life I developed some viewpoints that are still with me today. The uniqueness of the situation was that there was a literal price for participating. That fuelled me to take full ownership of my education for the first time in my life.

HUSSAIN: Is that when you started acting, at Poly?

DANNY: I read a ton of acting books during the year while I was at NYU Poly and then I transferred to NYU Tisch. The acting world was so new to me, I looked at everything with a magnifying glass. I started to break everything down intellectually, artistically, creatively and in the abstract. I started pursuing acting later than everyone else. I needed to play by different rules. I pursued it like a mad man knowing that my mum had put herself in a financial hole.

I became ritualistic around my acting process in my own way. I didn't want to be tied to an ideology. I took different tools from different philosophies and picked it apart and created my own.

HUSSAIN: Wow, thanks for breaking that down for us and giving us the insight. You've been on an incredible journey, what's been helping you recently?

DANNY: I've been speaking to my therapist lately (he's dope) and what had previously helped me through my entire life has been me saying, 'it's me against the world'. And the byproduct of that, when it wasn't against me, was that it still felt like it was, because a part that nobody teaches you is at one point the world isn't necessarily against you and you realise maybe it never was.

HUSSAIN: Tell me a bit about your healing process.

DANNY: The healing process has been to develop awareness around when out of muscle memory or necessity I put things in front of my own way. Because in all honesty, I never really trusted when things were easy. Turns out many people feel the same way.

Therefore a big thing that we've been talking about around healing is getting to a place where there's more agency and control over my mindset. And I've chosen to put up less resistance. And that doesn't necessarily mean comfortable.

HUSSAIN: Not to be a therapist, but can you unpack that?

DANNY: I had borrowed so much of my mentality from role models in the sports world, where there's a huge idea of not getting comfortable. For a while I had connected that to the feeling the world is against me, but now I'm glad to say I'm in a lot more control over it. I now dictate when I put myself in uncomfortable positions with how much work I put into my craft, skills I learn, gym, reading, work and love I put into relationships in my life.

HUSSAIN: Damn, Danny, you are doing a lot of work I hope to start doing!

DANNY: I then became fascinated with the exploration of myself and once I had the language of life, I really saw the time you spend on something does matter. Once I became a big believer in the 10,000 hours of mastery, I started loading up on books and started watching everything I could. From movies, YouTube to live plays, now my shelves are full of books. The only books I had ever read were assigned to me, none were from my own free will. Until I started acting. I have now read over 120 books over the last ten years.

HUSSAIN: And now you're in one!

DANNY: That's crazy.

HUSSAIN: I'm guessing it's fair to say books hugely impacted your life?

DANNY: So much, especially when combined with real life experiences. Not just intellectualising it but really living it. We met during a time where I was grieving the loss of my dad and I didn't really know I was preparing for it until I thought back on some books that have impacted me. One of them was *The Year of Magical Thinking* by Joan Didion. That book and therapy has given me a safe space to discover how I grieve. Seeing her grieve in her unique way gave me the freedom to do so in mine. Reading has been one of the biggest discoveries throughout this entire process.

HUSSAIN: Sorry for the loss of your dad. It's empowering to hear you speak.

DANNY: I appreciate you man.

HUSSAIN: A huge shoutout to Jay Ellis for introducing us and also Greg Tarzan Davis, the night we met you before the *Top Gun* premiere in London I am glad we got to celebrate you all by giving you your flowers.

DANNY: Thank you for celebrating us the moment we were achieving something, that was really impactful. Up until that point I only celebrated once the coast was clear. Celebrating the moment something was happening always felt premature or like it could get taken away, but those flowers that day shifted my perspective. Celebrate and if it gets taken away at least you get to smell the flowers.

HUSSAIN: In this case literally! We had to get you flowers, what you are all achieving is incredible. Last question, is there anyone you want to give flowers to through this book?

DANNY: My mom . . . duh!

Change The Journey, Not The Destination
MARYAM PASHA

Storyteller

Dear Maryam,

It's me. Or rather, it's you from the future. As you graduate and get started on your career I wanted to share with you something it has taken me almost twenty years to understand. It's about quitting. We're about to turn forty and in all those years, what you've come to realise is that your problem isn't that you're a quitter. Your problem is that you're *not*.

You find it really difficult to tell the difference between changing the journey and giving up on the destination.

You don't give up easily. You don't let people down casually. Those are good traits, and ones that others value in you. But sometimes it can and will be to your detriment. The first job you'll get once you finish all your studies is at a big NGO. Great, right?! That's your dream! But when you get there, you'll struggle. You'll have been there for a year and a half, and your work will be good, but it's hard being at that organisation, hard working with your supervisor, hard working within the wider culture, hard working in a silo, not integrated into the team, feeling like you're totally out of step. More than once you'll have to fight back tears in a meeting, you'll face racism and sexism and no one will believe you. But, despite all that, you'll feel lucky to be there. Grateful for the job. So when your contract comes to an end you ask for an extension without even considering any alternatives. Your boss's boss, who you got on with rather well, will instead sit you down and tell you that they're not renewing your contract, that this isn't the right place for you. It'll be devastating. You *know* you don't fit in, that you're not being enabled to do the work you're capable of, that the structure of the organisation isn't supporting you to thrive, but you'd never have left on your own, because you don't quit.

I wish this was the moment that you learn when to walk away. But you don't. Because you've got dreams and goals, and you think that walking away from this job would mean giving those up.

You continue to develop your intuition about people, places and things, but you can't bring yourself to listen to it, because sometimes it's telling you to get out of there and you're not a quitter, right? You tolerate toxic workplaces, relationships, social situations because you're loyal, because you've made a commitment, because you've said you'll do the thing. You keep committing to the same journey over and over because you think it'll help you reach your destination.

In your thirties, you'll take the leap to become self-employed, something you've always wanted to do but been too cautious to try. Once you decide to go out on your own, you'll think you have to prove yourself by working with big name brands. Craving this recognition as part of establishing yourself will mean you keep finding yourself in situations where your skills, your knowledge, all the things you're bringing to the table won't be properly valued, but of course you'll stay out of obligation. You'll stay because you think you need their validation, even though you *knew* from the first day or the third meeting that it was never going to be a productive relationship. You'll spend precious time and energy trying to figure out how to be the person they want you to be, and what you need to do to be treated better.

And all of this isn't to say that you should walk away at the first sign of difficulty or conflict. You don't want to become someone who lets the pendulum swing too far in the other direction, becoming a person who thinks they never need to learn how to deal with difficult people or difficult situations. But learn to read the signals, learn to listen to what people are telling you, rather than believing you have the personal willpower and strength to make every bad situation into a good one. The truth is that you can still get to where you want to go, you might just have to take a different route to get there.

Some of the best advice you ever get: learn how to recognise if the ground you find yourself in is fertile. Sometimes it doesn't matter what you do, nothing will ever grow. You're in a desert. And if you keep trying to plant your seeds in a desert, if you keep toiling away, not only will they not grow but you'll become so frustrated and distracted by the futility of what you're doing that you'll become a person you don't want to be: meaner, grumpier, more impatient. That's another clue: if you start acting in a way that just doesn't feel like you, maybe the environment you're in is not serving you.

It sounds defeatist but, I promise you, it's *not* about giving up on things you want. It's not about losing sight of your end goal or about the impact you want to have in the world. It's about being able to take a step back and figure out if this particular route is really going to get you there. It's about looking at this patch of land you've found yourself on and trying to establish if the seeds you're planting are ever going to grow. Are you in a garden or a desert?

What I hope you come to learn, faster than I did, is that you're not an imposter. You haven't fooled anyone into thinking you're better than you are. No one is going to realise one day that you've snuck into a job you don't deserve. Looking back, I can now see how feeling so unworthy and feeling like I didn't belong was the fuel to so much of this behaviour. I feared that if I left, there would be nowhere for me to go, no one who would want to work with me. That if I quit, everything I had worked so hard for would be over. This is simply not true – because the hard work, the determination and the skills you've spent so long working on will be cherished and valued elsewhere. This isn't about being more self-confident or getting over your imposter syndrome – the problem isn't you. There are so many times in our life where places and people have made us feel small and out of place – too Brown, too poor, too fat, too opinionated – we never really fit in. But the right lesson to take away from this, that I now know, is that it made us resilient and it gave us the confidence to walk into any room and any space and make our own way, instead of waiting for others to let us in.

So as you start out on what will be an amazing career, I want you to know something that has taken me almost twenty years to learn: sometimes the thing you're doing today is holding you back from the bigger thing you will do tomorrow. Quitting today's job, today's relationship or today's project might be an essential part of not giving up on tomorrow's.

Changing the journey does not have to mean changing the destination.

Love,
Maryam

Serpents Are Cold

ANONYMOUS

I had finally made it. Ecstatic. Proud and ready to support others to make their dreams a reality. The pinnacle of my career, leading a multimillion-pound business for minimal personal financial gain, but entrusted to develop the next generation, socially, emotionally and academically.

Over twenty successful years in my industry, built on the struggles growing up, life lessons that are worth their weight in gold. Social media messages from the people I met on my journey; overwhelming like the public and unconditional love of a grandmother.

A valuable necessity to me and society. The first person to ever look like me to reach such a height, it was a moment I will never forget.

Time multiplies gratitude.

I climbed that mountain, pushed by family and friends in cosmopolitan London. Celebrated by many in my diverse network and community. Pushed, pushed and pushed. Even Uncle Des raised his Red Stripe`*` to celebrate me.

The mountain was a struggle but never once did I give in to dark temptations. The rats 'bit and hit' to sell their poison but morals and the weight of expectation were enough to be forceful and headstrong to continue on my positive path. I must help 'good' and support others to be 'good'.

*Red Stripe is a Caribbean beer

I believe and preach equality of rights and opportunity to thousands. Be focused and work hard. But where did I become so naive? Is it not obvious that the top of that mountain would be slippery and cold? How quickly my ideals were stolen, through venomous bites from those who claim diversity to be important, but really do just use it, use me, use us, as a tick-box exercise. Those privileged smiling serpents; they are coiled symmetrical, their hiss would stun me still, so they can scrutinise our differences, disrupting the momentum.

Privilege is real and when it meets entitlement in numbers, you are on your own. And when you climb up the ladder from a working class background you really learn fast the term 'allies' for some is just a word, and for others who are willing to stick their name by yours, pay the cost of their careers.

My family: my sanctuary of happy loving faces, but every day leaving to re-enter the bear pit.

Isn't my birthplace *Great* Britain? The land of hope and opportunity, destroyed by those abusing their power. A selfish society created by those commanding high salaries and pretending to be too busy to even listen to my pleas.

Let them write their books on diversity and social mobility, making more money for themselves. Practice is not what is being preached. Glass ceilings are real but I am encased in a glass box now.

Caught between the rock of establishment and a hard place of reality.

I am hopeful that change is coming, change is here and that change will come, but I'm now exasperated; I'm too bruised to act. Angry, sore and unwell. Keep smiling and hope good will win.

Rock bottom now, but that is the strongest place to rebuild.

Nearest to home.

So to continue the struggle.

Note: The fact that I can't mention who I am tells you everything even when this is my truth, but I will not give up.

Duckling Watching From The Wings
KIRAN SONIA SAWAR

Actor

Spotlight shines on her head.
And from the wings,
I choose not to enter the scene tonight.
I watch instead.

How many times can a secondary character speak the same
　　lines?
10 times a night.
8 days a week.
'Are you alright?'

Costumes tight around my neck.
Line check. Tech-nique.

She mumbles her first line. Her second. Her third, the favourite
　　and this one sublime.
Rehearsed delivered Devine.
Cuts through the audience.

This line was mine.

The acts are awash with memories. Bridge-threatening, plane-
　　deafening trips to the seaside.

Play ends. Drama begins.

As we wait for the dressing room reviews:
I watch the beads of sweat fall from her make-up'd head. She
    doesn't know.
She pre-empts the impending news:

'It's all lose lose'

And 'Oh' how she acts the reaction.
A clapper board in action.

The reprise.
And surprise surprise, I'm a duckling back in the wings.
Plucked feathers.
My attention falls on the selfless crew
The managing theatre managers and their endless lists.

She'll always be number one. And my name doesn't even exist

Don't Get Too High With The Highs, Or Too Low With The Lows

MARO ITOJE

Rugby Union player, athlete, founder of Pearl Fund

Playing a sport that is reasonably popular, you open yourself up to a certain amount of criticism, but conversely you also give yourself the opportunity to receive a high amount of praise if you perform well or if you do well or if the team is successful. And I believe that both sides of the coin have the potential to be equally dangerous. When you are in a situation where you are doing well, on top of the world and everyone is loving you and praising you, if you allow that to get inside your head it can be quite disorientating in the sense that it can influence the way you think, the way you behave, the way you act in negative ways.

You can start thinking that your sh*t doesn't smell, or that you're too good, or that all the success is due to you, and when that happens that can also lead to potentially you not working as hard as you were before. You are not grinding quite as hard as you were before. And that is the potential risk with success, you can lose your desire and lose your hunger.

On the other side of the coin with criticism, if you are totally swayed by the criticism you receive in your life, then you will have no control over your emotions, you will be a slave to what other people say about you. If people say good things about you, you feel good; if people say bad things about you, you feel bad. You have no control over your life and it can make you down and a little bit depressed. And what I mean when I say 'it's never as good or it's never as bad as it seems' is when you are going through those positive periods in your life it's very often the hyperbole and the rhetoric around you that it's not as good as what people are saying. Most of the time that tends to be true, and often when you go through loss, when you go through criticism, when you go through down periods, it's often the rhetoric that is a lot more negative than what people are saying as well. So with that, it's never really as bad as you feel and it's never really as good as you feel.

I like to have this philosophy as it helps regulate my emotions and helps keep me in control of how I am feeling as opposed to the highs and lows that come with professional sport. I learnt this over time. In my career I have had a lot of praise, probably more than most, and I have also had periods where I've had a little bit of criticism as well, especially when the team hasn't been performing to the level we expect. And often when you get that praise you feel good, but if you take that for granted and believe everything they say, you are taking your eye off the ball.

Conversely, when I have had criticism I know what they are saying is not totally true. I also heard T.I. say a phrase on this on 'expediTIously with Tip T.I. Harris', *'If you live for the cheers, you will die by their boo's'.* I also remember with regards to criticism, he said, *'You can't let someone who doesn't have all the information about you, decide on how you're feeling.'* He talked about how no one else knows every single thing about you or everything that's happening in your life, so you can't let other people dictate your actions or emotions.

I believe people who you trust and there's people whose opinions you respect depending on what it is.

Let's say it's in a rugby context; the opinions that matter to me are my coaches' opinions and my teammates' opinions and maybe a few trusted advisors in and around rugby. They are the opinions that matter to me. It's the people who I trust, the people who are good at what they do; as a result they can offer an informed opinion on what I am doing.

Most of the time with criticism there's probably an element of truth in it somewhere, so it's not as if it's all rubbish, so it's about understanding what the root cause of the issue is and trying to dissect it. I think being open to feedback and having a growth mindset is very important, that way you can continue to improve and carry on getting better. If you don't have a growth mindset you cut yourself off from any form of feedback and I believe feedback is important for all of us with whatever avenue you are in.

It's important to keep the main thing, the main thing. Kobe Bryant said it once: '*Whether you win or lose, you are going back to the work, the process after that,*' so everything is about the process, it's all about self-improvement, and getting better while striving to achieve something.

I think it's really helpful to be surrounded by like-minded individuals. I've been really fortunate throughout my career to be surrounded by people of that mindset, people who want to get better, who want to push things, people who want to try to take things to the next level.

And the reality of the situation is the minute you start resting on your laurels is the minute you start to decline in whatever you do, especially in sport; the levels are always increasing, the standards are always getting higher, so if you're not continuing to push it, you're going to fall behind . . .

Blessings & Lessons

TYLER WEST

TV and radio presenter

I can't tell you the number of times I've read, listened to or been told the words 'never give up'. Whether that's a sign above your 'live, laugh, love' friend's toilet or on a TikTok of some American chat show that your group chat sent you to feel ten seconds of motivation. But the truth is life certainly isn't linear and it's much easier said than done. There's no straight route from A to B and what works for you might not work for someone else, but the journey to discover what works is what I've found, major key. It's in the journey where you will learn about yourself, what you want, options present themselves and you just figure it out. (Nobody knows EXACTLY the right way, but the only way you get closer to that answer is by trying).

For me it comes down to a few fundamentals. The main one being *how willing you are*, how far you are prepared to go, doing whatever it takes to get there. An old mentor of mine when I first started in my industry explained my goals to me as the London tube map. Just say for example your usual route to where you need to get to on the Central line has major delays . . . Okay fine, I'll take my car. Your car has a flat tyre . . . Okay fine, I'll cycle. Ah, bikes are banned for some reason . . . Okay never mind, I'll walk. The fact is there is always a WAY to get there, but it all starts with you and how much you *want* to get there.

Making the decision to give your all to something will either bring you blessings or lessons. Imagine driving down a road, getting to the traffic lights, not knowing whether to go left, right or just continue being indecisive and going straight on. Eventually you will have no choice but to turn left or right. And whichever way you choose, you are guaranteed to 1. Learn if it was the right decision. 2. Do a U-turn/reroute if it wasn't. That is literally the *worst that could happen*. The minute you actively withdraw the fear of going wrong, that 'big' goal, challenge or aspiration of yours becomes more achievable.

Sometimes the idea of 'never giving up' seems a harder feat than actually doing it. We pre-empt the bad outcomes, let our fears take over and doubt ourselves. Any time I feel this happening with me, my goals or aspirations, I like to think of it as a 'fuck it' moment. If it's something that scares you and challenges you, it means you care. Pluck up the courage to say 'fuck it' and give it a go. You will surprise yourself every single time.

These are just some of the fundamentals that helped me. Because if I rewind, the man I was is the polar opposite to the man I am today. I would've laughed in your face if you had told me I'd be doing the things I do today. Along my journey were several hurdles and moments so that giving up seemed the only viable option. However, having the determination to power through, using my past as my fuel, and giving my all to the opportunities that come my way, is the reason I am still going, and trust me: if I'm still going, you certainly can keep going too.

Dear Discrimination
HUSSAIN MANAWER

My career has blessed me in an abundance of ways, through experiences, connections, feelings and lessons, all of which I would never have encountered without poetry. I am incredibly grateful and thankful for all of this. However, what comes with this unfortunately or should I say fortunately is the following. Something I have never ever spoken of publicly, but now is more vital than ever for me to do so, is the discrimination I have so publicly faced in scenarios and settings.

Sometimes, being the only person who looks like you, that has a name like yours, in the rooms and spaces you are in, really leads to a wild adventure of experiences . . .

Within the past few months alone in 2023 the following experiences have happened:

- Entering a taxi and the taxi driver asking me if I am a terrorist . . . (this was not banter)

- Being invited to a high-profile event as a guest and being asked to make a black coffee by another guest, as they thought I was catering staff

- Not being spoken to, looked past and being made to feel invisible in work settings, then having other friends and colleagues ask me what just happened (bruh)

- Being *constantly* stopped at airports across the world (due to random searches) – I now factor in hours of time to travel due to this and have really learnt to stay calm and relaxed in these settings.

I then found, eventually this began to wear me down, over years and years of me internalising and normalising these microaggressions and unconscious biases. I lost the fight and would find myself crying by myself. I didn't want to tell my family, or my friends, I didn't want them to worry as this along with life, grief, barriers of entry and everything else going on in the world is just something that doesn't need to be addressed. But I found after speaking to my close friends and family about it, it most certainly does. I found myself writing a letter, one I wanted to share with you all here.

Dear Discrimination,

I am really not sure who invited you to my party, but here you are. You are definitely not one to come empty-handed.

Through all the trials and tribulations, tests and dirty trenches you have thrown and dragged me through somehow I am still here and I am still going. This is the thing Discrimination you really don't seem to understand; before you would be a thing that eats at me and now with a lifetime of having you and your energy around, guess what, your tactics no longer work.

Every time you appear in a social setting and un-see me and my friends, your weak pathetic attempt to make us feel invisible only shines us brighter in a sea amongst your own facade.

Every time you laugh and joke at our expense, you are only

further weakening the ties of the friendships you think you are growing with those you are conversing with.

Every time you attempt to trick me out of a position with a smile, I hate to break it to you, but you fail.

Every time you make me work a million times harder, make me question my sanity and dance with the fine line of depression, you have done nothing but bring me closer to having real conversations, on earnest levels, and have helped me strengthen the relationships in my life.

Here is the thing you have not realised: I am not the only one who is now behaving like this. There are many of us, many of us who are now turning you into something. So many of us are joining forces, finding hope, peace and understanding through the look in our eyes because you have given us something.

Something you believed for so long was going to drive us away or in some cases insane, but that something we have found in isolation leads us to then finding peace, finding solitude and also finding understanding.

And if that wasn't enough we then now find the bricks and capacity to cement these bricks to collectively build bridges that can withstand you and all of your gaslighting nonsense. To not only help ourselves but each other.

It's becoming funny, because the confidence that I am now feeling when having experienced your wickedness empowers me beyond my wildest imagination. Because for a very long while, you were very successful in tricking me into thinking I wasn't worthy of being in the rooms and spaces I am now in.

Let's break down this a little bit more shall we? Discrimination is another form of intimidation. When you are in a position be it at work for example and you are being discriminated against, and your friends and family are out living their lives and have their own stuff going on, it's not as easy as it once was to pick up the phone and explain a situation to someone you love to receive that comfort.

Discrimination is poisonous and the remedy to it is continuing to shine your light and to speak about it. Sometimes I really understand we shine sad and we want to shout and sometimes we shine while we cry, while we attend to our broken parts, internalising and carrying so much within.

But regardless we are still shining; even if you are unaware, your presence automatically reflects back on what tried to tear you down and if you look a little closer, you can notice the cracks, their insecurities, the over-projection, the lack of talent, inability to access humility, peace of mind, the whole works (and this is not your problem to fix fyi).

Discrimination, please come to my next party, don't forget to take your shoes off, I've got so many friends I can't wait to introduce you to, because, just like me, we've all done the work and we are not going to be scared into paving career paths, roads, ways forward, because it's not just for us, there's an entirely new generation coming straight after.

Looks like tonight we will be dancing to the rhythm of our own growth.

All The Shade,
Hussain

I'm Still Going

HUSSAIN MANAWER

You can't give up now,
You've come to far
So don't even entertain the thought
No, listen to me, you've come too far
From this point, your never be looking back

Growing older
The game really does take time
It kills me seeing my niece grow up on facetime
Imposter syndrome you can keep, it aint mine
I blew up on the spot – the lands mine

Gotta get the words right i'm playing hang time
too many pretty faces with bad minds
I don't like the state of humanity
Trapped in a cell,
Now I'm asking, why aint man-kind?

Hustling hard
The golden state
Summer hours
in a dark hole
oblivion at alton towers
If I rate you and your alive

One thing from me, I'll make sure you get your flowers
Nazar is real
Evil eye has got its powers
Doctor evil . . .
Someone call up Austin Powers
I'm here to make something mine
The maddest thing is - it was never ours

Sometimes your own community can be the worst
Secretly praying for your down fall
Nothing positive to say when something good happens
But when something negative happens all of a sudden it's
funny how everyone's got a mouthful
I've been doing this since I was 15
I remember taking the central line from Gants Hill
Just so I can perform open mics in Southall

If I stopped to fight every battle
I would have never got through the airport
There Causing me a racket
I'm not tennising on their court
My citizens can't get the ship
Won't let them pass, them at their ports
Too hungry
There's no food round here
For their thoughts
There pulling on my heartstrings
I'm never been into half things
Now I Understand
Why Sinatra went to palm springs
I'm Taking care of my family
Looking after me has really become the last thing

My lifestyles – emotional
Photos on disposables
Introverted, extroverted, socially, unsociable
I've always been approachable
In a game that's unconsolable
I'm a wizard with these words
Out here fighting these Voldermorts

None of these lot writ me
Singing along to Whitney
I got my heart smashed, and then discovered the hits me
I found the writing on wall when they never picked me
I'm studying this Mickey
Uncle Larry tells me it's history

I'm still stuck up in a mystery
Trying to figure out
How has my passion become manufactured out of misery

Hold

COLIN SALMON

Father, actor, friend

Give up? . . . I
Started this so many times
Have drafted so many openings
So many different endings.
Debated fonts and font sizes.
Whether it was to be allegorical, autobiographical, fictional or
    factual
Poetic, stoic, even political.
A look at my childhood, adulthood, maybe my middle hood
Dare I share my present hood?
Should it be funny in tone or serious insight,
Light or intense, with or without a moral?
Echo my heritage, reflect a select tragic history or be
    aspirational and full of hope
To help inspire with stories of glories and conquest?
Write for a specific audience or allow it to find its own
    audience?
Do I actually need an audience?
Should I just write it for myself?

Today or maybe tomorrow
I've got some time next week
Actually it is nearly the end of the month so that could fly.
Have some paid work to do first though

Don't want to miss out for a freebie
But it's important and don't want to let a brother down
True that you know
So let's get to it.

Hang on there's the phone!
I know it it's not ringing
I'm sure there's something interesting to look at
Of course I have to do my chess puzzles religiously
Up my game
In case I do actually play somebody face to face one day.

Of course I'm going to get it done though
Send it to my bro
Because I know
I need to show
Him, myself and the world
. . . what exactly?

This inside us dialogue of
Someone who wants to do the right thing
Second guessing themselves on every stage
Until they feel frozen standing at the abyss.

When that feeling comes

Breathe

Hold

It doesn't make you a bad person even though they may feel
    like a bad person

Useless, waste man, stupid, broken, ineffective, whatever
All the other household labels you find stacked high on the
    shelves of
The low self-esteem superstore . . . add to that the one-off
    special 'Hopeless'
and you're suddenly struggling with the weak, bulging plastic bags
The handles will always snap and spill with the classics 'What's
    the point.'
Or 'I didn't want to do it anyway.'
(Note these classics come with added expletives can result in
    seething misdirected intent, blame and malice.)
Terms and conditions applied.
You don't have to shop there.
The friend asked for your help because they know you can do
    it.
You have the ability to deliver in your own time
Make time and space in your day, your heart and your mind
Just allow it (love that term), engage with it and quietly
    complete it.
Speak it, sing it, question it, listen for it, text it, just simply
    record it

It may not be smooth, clever, insightful or even very good,
    whatever that is?
But it can be honest and that is enough.
Speak your truth
Others speak their truth
They cannot totally reflect you
But their words can affect you
Create an emotional response in you
Even render you speechless.
If that happens to you

Say nothing

Breathe

Hold

Allow yourself time because you can handle it
You already know all things pass
Therefore you don't ever need to Give Up
Much more effective

To get up, pass up, let up, tone up, love up, tune up, wise up,
    look up,
Or maybe
Take up, run up, gear up, wrap up, tear up, eat up, drink up, live
    up . . .

Peace Up

PART THREE

Hope

COURTENEY COX

MISHA B

MATT EAGLES

JAMES SMITH

ZINNIA KUMAR

JACK HARRIES

HAMZAH SHEERAZ

BUNMI MOJEKWU

HERO FIENNES TIFFIN

BEN SHEPHARD

JASPREET KAUR

RYAN ADAGIO WINCH

JEREMY VINE

RYAN KEEN

DAN DARE

HUSSAIN MANAWER

JORDAN STEPHENS

GREG TARZAN DAVIS

EMMA HEDILE AL-MUNSHI

GIAN POWER

BRADY CAMPBELL

ANONYMOUS

CHIDERA EGGERUE AKA THE SLUMFLOWER

It's A Long Fall From California To Alabama
COURTENEY COX

Actress

Early on in my career, when I barely made any money, I used to count exactly how many weeks, months or days I had left to live in California if I didn't get a job. I would ask my accountant who was helping me, 'Exactly how much time do I have to be able to stay in Los Angeles?' So, it's 1987, I'm twenty-three years old and it has gotten down to my final month. I had around three weeks left, I'm down to the wire. I'm talking to my dad on the phone and I remember him saying: 'CC, it's a long fall from California to Alabama, you need to come home and do what you do best . . . sell swimming pools!'

Which is the business my dad was in. He continued:

'You're a damn good salesman, you always have been. It's time that you came back to Birmingham and sold swimming pools!'

My reply was: 'Dad, I don't want to come back, there's nothing wrong with Alabama, but that's not my dream . . . to be a swimming pool salesman.'

Even though I worked in a swimming pool store during high school, and I AM a really good salesman, that's beside the point.

I couldn't wrap my head around it, I was so depressed. But then literally the next day, twenty-four hours later, I got a call saying that I had booked the job on *Family Ties*. It was like a miracle. I didn't have to fall from Los Angeles (even though it's straight across to Birmingham) after all. Looking back to that period, I was really working out fear. I didn't understand what manifesting was. Now I really know how important words are, what we put out into the universe.

During that period, I never thought like that. I'm very self-deprecating, putting myself down in jest or not. I'm now realising that is not the right thing to do. We need to put out positive thoughts. Manifest as if it has already happened, that is my new way of doing things.

Looking back, I see how fear kept me from taking chances that I should have. I feel really fortunate that I didn't have to go back home to sell swimming pools, even though there's nothing wrong with that – sorry Dad!

I love acting, I love directing, I love producing, I love any part of the creative process in this business. But also, I am a happier, more adventurous person now. I even created my homecare line, called Homecourt. I'm a lot more passionate, I take more chances and I don't just hope things will work out. I don't believe in 'No's'. I don't mind '*I don't know,*' but I don't believe in No's.

I don't like to sit still, I'm constantly moving, seriously I don't sit down the whole day and if I do sit down, the only thing that keeps me there is if one of my dogs is sitting on my lap.

I'm a curious person, I get bored pretty easily, I just want to keep changing and growing. I'm always on the go and I really do believe if there's a will there's a way.

The Fire Within

MISHA B

Artist, musician and dear friend

I often fall in love with moments
Places, people and things
Love sees no class, no race, no ego
It serves both the pauper and the king
Few and many times I've wondered
Has love passed me by?
But I have searched and I have found
I Am where **Love** resides

50 Years Living With Parkinson's
MATT EAGLES

Positivity activist

My name is Matt.

I am a positivity activist.

I have Parkinson's.

Not that unusual, I am sure you would agree. Middle-aged, white, male – surely the absolute stereotypical Parky man according to Dr Google!

However, if I told you I was diagnosed with this chronic, degenerative neurological disease on my seventh birthday, it would probably come as a bit of a surprise. Not an ideal present, particularly as my preference was a bicycle!

Despite the average age of diagnosis being seventy-plus, people can live with the early signs for many years without seeking medical advice or without knowing anything untoward is happening to them.

REM sleep disturbances, excessive tiredness, apathy, depression, balance issues, problems emptying your bowels or an urgency to pee, micrographia (small handwriting) and a hand tremor are some of the more common ones, but there are over forty recognised symptoms and not all manifest at the same time.

I do consider myself to be very lucky though; I cannot remember NOT having Parkinson's so everything I have managed to achieve, I have done so despite it. I have nothing to compare my life with, it has been an ever present in my life.

The fact is I didn't choose Parkinson's, rather it chose me.

Ideally, I wanted to be the next Jacques-Yves Cousteau and sail the seas looking after marine life, but circumstances conspired against me. It's a double blow really as I'm a lifelong West Ham United fan and that hasn't been easy either.

I am now in a unique position to be able to pass on my experience and knowledge, not only of living with Parkinson's but also the communication difficulties PWP face daily.

I like to believe I will change the way you can live with a chronic neurological illness by promoting positivity while not forgetting the seriousness of the condition.

Parkinson's disease can and indeed does control every aspect of my daily life, from waking up in the morning writhing about like a newly caught fish on a river bank to trying to make my way to the bathroom to go for a wee like the scarecrow trying to reach Oz down the yellow brick road – yes, I am aware scarecrows cannot wee, but stick with me on this.

Showering becomes an Olympic discipline, a kind of crazy dance as my body twerks awkwardly to the cascade of water as I grip the safety rail attached to the stubborn tiled wall. To the uninitiated it might look like I'm practising for a stint on *Strictly Come Dancing*. I can assure everyone I'm not!

Falling off the bed while trying to put on my undies, one leg in and one leg out, has become a particular favourite pastime of mine. Not very dignified, but rather amusing to watch according to my wife.

Each room in the house, each transition between rooms, is fraught with risk.

The kitchen in particular is full of danger. I break crockery while washing up and drying dishes. I cannot move pans on the gas hob for fear of burning myself and sending the contents of the pan all over the floor. I cannot use a kettle; we now have a water boiler. When making a cup of coffee, I spill the coffee, then the milk, then once the cup is full, I often spill that too, forcing me to start all over again!

Every single task most people do every day without even thinking can become my Everest. It's never-ending!

It's super difficult to answer our landline without my ear inadvertently ending the call prematurely.

Typing on a keyboard, holding a book, taking selfies for social media posts, can all at times be beyond me. Even trying to do up shoelaces is a nightmare, and trying to eat sometimes just becomes impossible as I cannot get the food onto the cutlery to put it in my mouth.

However . . .

This is my everyday – and all the above can be incredibly frustrating and stressful, but I then ask myself this question. 'Did I choose to have Parkinson's. Is it my fault? Does it help to get angry and upset about every little mishap or fall?'

The answer of course is NO!

Many times, I've sat on my bottom in our galley kitchen, my t-shirt and trousers soaked by a tidal wave of dirty washing-up water that has leapt over the lip of the stainless seal lip of the sink, broken crockery looking like oversized croutons in a soapy soup surrounding me on the floor, wondering how ridiculous this must look to a casual bystander. It makes me smile and helps me cope. It was also the spark I needed to put together my wellness programme for the Parkinson's Community – Parkylife, the brighter side of Parkinson's! – to help others to cope with their diagnosis and to give them hope.

Thank You Mum x

JAMES SMITH

Musician

My story goes back to my childhood. I was brought up around the London Borough of Newham. We lived in my nan's council flat in Upton Park, which actually looked over the West Ham football ground (a huge bonus). Me and my brother were smart kids, so my parents worked ridiculous hours in the hope that they could send us to better secondary schools. It was when we moved out of my nan's into our own house in Essex that my whole world changed. It seemed like there was so much opportunity. Everyone had money and the public schools were as good as the private ones. I remember my mum writing letters to the schools and making me go to every single club in the area so that I had more of a chance of getting a place at one of them. Fast forward a couple of months of trying and trying, I got a place. My family was over the moon.

The school was great. I, however, was not. It was a foreign environment to me. I was uncomfortable and felt like I needed to prove myself all the time. I played up, got into fights, and eventually got myself expelled. As a young kid, it was probably the worst thing that I could have done. I let my mum down after all that hard work she did. I let myself down. All the other families in the area didn't want their kids hanging out with me and no other schools would take me. I became a loner. In the period of time that I was out of school, I had to work on a market stall in Upton Park; back to where I started. I suppose it doesn't sound so bad looking back on it, but honestly, it was a traumatic moment for all of us.

I was about thirteen at this point and, on my journey into work, I would listen to music. This was when I discovered the greats in music like Bob Dylan and Stevie Wonder. I remember wanting to be like them so bad but it seemed entirely unachievable because of my situation. However I thought to myself that I needed to stop wallowing in my own pity and do something. I somehow found the nerve to start singing songs for the market traders at work. I remember the blokes telling my mum that she should be proud, and she was. She helped me get gigs. I started in pubs, which led to clubs, which led to small venues, which led to me now working on my debut album, headlining shows around Europe. I'm still on my journey, but I'm so glad that I chose to not give up. And I am forever grateful to my mum.

You Could Be A Scientist If You Wanted

ZINNIA KUMAR

Model, activist and storyteller

I thought 'hope' would be the most fitting for my story. My name is Zinnia Kumar, I was born in Sydney, Australia and now live in London. I'm a model, activist and storyteller.

I come from an underprivileged community. The year I graduated, I attended the lowest-ranked school in the state of NSW, Australia.

I was constantly told from society that I would never amount to anything, with no encouragement, no role models or empowerment. I thought I was not smart enough to get into university, let alone ever dream of working in media, having never seen anyone that looked like me. I'd settled on being a rubbish truck driver as I felt I could help the environment in some way.

One day my science teacher kept me back after class. I was convinced I was in trouble! Instead, she sat opposite me, looked me in the eye and told me, 'Zinnia, you know you can be anything, you could be a scientist if you wanted.' I had a lump in my throat, no words would come out; nobody ever looked at me and said anything like that. It was at that moment I realised that sometimes you need someone to start that journey for you, to believe in you, before you can believe in yourself.

Through her words she planted a powerful seed, and slowly I started to believe and to find a way out. With only hope, I self-learnt courses in the library. Through hard work I went from the lowest-ranked school to the world's best universities (Oxford and UCL). Originally working three jobs to make ends meet in London, a chance encounter with a model scout on Tottenham Court Road gave me the opportunity to be financially independent, a platform to reach more people and a space for other South Asians to see someone from their community work in fashion. After all, racial visibility normalises the historical 'other' and creates harmonious communities.

Meanwhile, I worked to fulfil my dream of becoming a scientist. Which I did eventually accomplish as a conservationist and now a researcher in consumer psychology, finding real-world solutions for sustainability and increasing South Asian representation in media and fashion.

However, something about that life-changing moment, when that fire was lit, became an obsession. I started working grassroots, doing workshops to empower disadvantaged young women in Australia, India and Thailand; I wanted them to know the key, that the student and not the school, where they come from, their social class or what they look like matters.

Empowerment is a moment in time, it's when the fire from within is lit. It is the moment when we reject imposed dogma and choose to believe in ourselves and our capability, to break the barrier.

Empowering hope is transformational. Two and a half years ago I met and started mentoring a girl, struck by her potential. I sat down with her, looked her in the eye, just as the teacher had done for me years ago and I said, 'You know you can be anything you want to be.' She's now at university, financially independent, shifting global South Asian beauty ideals, she is a carer for her father with cancer and a role model and mentor for girls within her community. Passing on the infectious baton of hope from one to another. Creating a wildfire of endless positivity.

A moment of hope can have a lifetime of impact. So, whoever needs to hear this, I see the flame within you, it doesn't matter where you have come from, what you look like or what you have been through, I believe in you.

Realigning With My Purpose
JACK HARRIES

Documentary film-maker and campaigner

I was twenty-three and I had everything. Since leaving school
at eighteen I'd been lucky enough to earn a living travelling the
world, making films and sharing them on the internet. On
social media, I had millions of followers, but inside I felt
desperately lonely. I should have been happy, but I wasn't. This
is my story of why I wanted to quit and the tools I used to
discover an alternative path.

My dream was always to become a film-maker. To
communicate, to tell stories, to connect with people and to see
the world. I had no idea how to get there or what a career
would even look like but a spontaneous decision to create a
YouTube channel – when I should have been revising for my A
levels – changed my life. I will never forget the look on my
parents' faces when my brother and I both announced we were
quitting university to make YouTube videos for a living. Let's
say they weren't best pleased, but, to their credit, they were
supportive of our ambitions to do something different, and so
cautiously they gave their blessing. Together with my brother
Finn, I built a YouTube channel called 'JacksGap', which grew to
an audience of four million people over the period of five
rollercoaster years. I look back on those years fondly. We had
the chance to be playful and creative and in the process see the
world and meet people from all walks of life. We discovered a
virtual universe of 'content creators' and together we

collaborated, creating videos, exploring new cultures and growing our audiences while riding the wave of a rapidly growing platform. At times it felt like being strapped to a rocket launcher. These were the early days of content creation on the internet, and terms like 'YouTuber' and 'influencer' (thankfully) didn't exist. Even the concept of making money from the internet felt new and novel. We were in the Wild West of a nascent digital video revolution and we were having the time of our life.

It was in 2015 when Finn decided he didn't want to carry on making films on the internet. To be honest he had never felt comfortable being on camera or receiving excessive amounts of attention. It's taken me a while to realise that while I'm a hopeless attention-seeker, Finn is really an introvert. Despite being identical twins, it's always been the case that while I recharge from being around people, Finn is more comfortable in his own company, often reading a daunting-looking book or academic paper. In many ways, this is why we worked so well together. We both had unique skills, which we combined to navigate our early YouTube years. But for Finn, the element of fame that accompanied our YouTube careers felt uncomfortable and unnatural. Ultimately he felt he had drifted far away from his own life's purpose and so one day, quite dramatically, he decided to apply for an architecture degree at a design school in New York City. He was accepted and in the summer of 2015 he left to essentially begin a new life on the other side of the Atlantic.

I wasn't prepared for how much this would impact me. I had only ever known twindom and suddenly singleton life felt very overwhelming and I suppose . . . lonely. While I was happy that he was pursuing his dreams, I found it difficult to continue creating videos and I realised that having Finn by my side was what gave me the confidence to do these ambitious things in the first place. With him gone I felt as though I'd lost a superpower. While I did my best to continue creating and sharing, inside I felt lost and alone. It was around this time that I broke up with my first significant girlfriend. We'd been together for four years but gradually drifted apart. These combined events left me feeling lost and disconnected. I no longer felt clear on my identity and purpose, both of which had been crucial drivers in my work since leaving school. A lot of that period of my life is a hazy blur.

In 2016 I was diagnosed with clinical depression for the first time in my life and prescribed antidepressants. Gradually my sharing of films on the internet ground to a halt and I began to feel very negative about everything I had done up until that point in my life. The thoughts and voice in my mind became very negative and self-critical. *'What have I actually achieved?'* *'I don't deserve any of this "success"'. 'Have I messed up Finn's life plan?' 'This is all my fault'. 'Is there any authenticity in what I'm making?'* and fundamentally . . . *'Why am I doing this?! – I don't feel happy!'* One of the beautiful things that first attracted me to YouTube was that it felt like a very authentic place. So if I could no longer be authentic with my audience then what did I have to offer? In other words, 'I WANTED TO QUIT'. I wanted out of everything. If only the world could have provided a black hole to swallow me up, I would have gladly disappeared. Instead, I receded into a thick cocoon of depression. I disconnected from the world. At times it felt like looking at the world through a hazy pane of glass. While I didn't feel happy, at least I felt safe. The irony of course is that this state of mind became a negative self-fulfilling prophecy that drove me further away from friends, family, happiness, creativity and fulfilment.

Looking back, there were many things that helped me get out of this place. Of course, it's easy to simplify this process in retrospect, and the truth is that it's a messy journey of ups and downs in which I'm still learning to quieten the mind, and come back to a place of self-love. A journey I've come to learn many of us navigate on a daily basis. A long motorcycle trip wild camping around Europe was a useful start, allowing me to disconnect from social media and reconnect with myself, nature and a sense of purpose. It was after that trip that I decided I wanted to commit myself to communicating more about the environment. Deep in my belly, I felt this was an important story to tell and one that would only become more prevalent throughout my lifetime. This renewed sense of purpose led me on a journey that ultimately saw me meet my future partner, go back to study – completing a master's in documentary film-making – start a new creative business, which I still run today, and ultimately come back to YouTube to create a twelve-part series featuring some of my heroes like Jane Goodall, David Attenborough and Barack Obama. *None of this* had seemed remotely possible just a few years before.

This year I'm going to turn thirty and it gives me great joy to say I feel more happiness than I have in a long time. I'm still with my partner and together we're building a life. I feel aligned with my purpose and most days – not all of them – I jump out of bed to start the day. I still have to commit rigorously to keeping my mental health in check. A combination of tools like regular exercise, yoga, meditation and breathwork help me stay balanced and present. A group of close friends who I trust and love hold me accountable and, in return, I endeavour to do the same for them. I suppose the lesson I've learnt in the ten years since leaving school is that purpose is *everything*. I think many young people are searching for that today. Especially in the frantic and disjointed world we all now live in. It feels like every day there's an existential threat to navigate. However, within every crisis, there is an opportunity to be part of the solution. The world is made of stories, and if they're not working it's up to us to tell new ones. Whatever change you want to see in the world my advice is this: find your unique gift that no one else has and lend that to the movement. I believe everyone has one. It doesn't matter whether it's big or small, humble or ambitious, loud or quiet, local or global. It's needed.

This Four-Letter Word

HAMZAH SHEERAZ

British boxer – WBO light middleweight champion

The other day I was thinking if I went back to school and I had to give a speech and I was looking at myself back then, and if I was that kid looking at me coming on to the stage, I thought, what would I say? Things came into my mind like work hard, stay dedicated, this and that and the other.

And do you know what I thought?

I wouldn't pay any attention to myself really and truly if I came on stage and said these things and saw that. I wouldn't pay attention at all.

So I was thinking about it when I was lying in bed during my training camp in May 2023 in Los Angeles, because when I'm on my own and I'm isolated I think a lot about things.

Now I'm thinking, thinking, what would I say? Then I went back to watching TV, then I came back to it, then I thought you know what it is, I thought every person in that room at the time must have something in common. What is that? And I thought, if we attach ourselves to something, we have hope. Four letters, H O P E.

So much comes down to hope. At the age of eight I got into boxing, this is how I made what I was thinking relevant to me. I said to myself: when I started boxing I was eight years old, I did it for fun, I was enjoying myself until the age of about sixteen. Then I worked an apprenticeship for about six months. I quit boxing. I thought this isn't what I was born to do. During

145

that time, I kept thinking to myself, this is not what I want to do, this is not what I want to do. So I then quit work and walked right back into the boxing gym.

I thought what is it I want to do? And I thought you know what, I want to take this seriously now. At the time I had no sponsors, nothing. Just myself, hard work and hope, literally.

That's what it all came down to, I thought, if I keep working hard, if I keep hoping, if I keep hold of these four letters, hope, who knows where it will take me . . .

The Security Guard
BUNMI MOJEKWU

Actress, friend and CEO of BAM Productions

The reason I don't give up is truly because I've tried and I wasn't able to do it. That's when I knew all my dreams were just memories of my future. There was a time, not long ago, when I was so down and I stayed down in my bed for days on end and all I could see was black. Sadness consumed me. My agent had called me for an audition and I just knew I couldn't not turn up again, so I gathered all the little I had and made my way into London. I honestly don't know how I arrived at the audition but I kept trying to read the script and nothing was registering. I went to the restroom and saw myself, a broken self, and finally burst into tears. In that bathroom stall I cried with no sound, I was numb. I walked into the room and gave a poor performance to prove I wasn't in pieces. I made my way back to my car and went to pay for my parking ticket. The security guard asked me what my name was, I said, 'Bunmi'. He then asked for my full name and I replied, 'Oluwabunmi'. He asked if I knew the meaning and I told him my name means God's gift. He looked me in the eye and said I should never forget that, that my name was given not by chance, that I have a gift and it is to be given. At that moment I felt light, a huge weight was lifted from me. He let me go free, another blessing I needed. I know everything I'm going through no matter how hard.

I am fully equipped to handle my pain. Life didn't stop kicking my butt but I know I have the tools I need to proceed. I try my hardest to think with a positive mind, even when I think . . . AGAIN! I know I have the power to create the life I want. I have a gift of art and a gift is to be shared. I encourage you reading this to stop right now and look around you and be grateful. Now take a breath. What is your name? Find the meaning or create one, so when you call on yourself you know exactly what you are putting out, and make sure it is exactly what you expect to receive, take another breath and remember giving up is not an option.

I Hope They Need It More Than I Do

HERO FIENNES TIFFIN

Actor and dear friend

When I was younger I played a small role in the Harry Potter films, so in my teenage years I had a bit of money I would spend on new football boots, video games etc. Through those years my older brother and his friends had a love for motorbikes and naturally I inherited that love, so as my sixteenth birthday was approaching I wanted to get a bike. At sixteen years old 50cc is the largest engine size you can get, but since I had already been riding bikes with my brother and his friends for years a 50cc was boring to me. But a bike is a bike and on my birthday I bought myself an Aprilia RS50. I loved it, but I could almost run faster than the bike and it was already falling to pieces the day I bought it.

A year later, I turned seventeen and could now legally ride a 125cc. I had ridden my RS50 into the ground. With about £3,000 left to my name I found the bike I wanted. It was the Alitalia edition of the Aprilia RS4 125. It was in great nick. The seller had listed it for £2,850 on Gumtree. I met him at his house in Mitcham and bought the bike on the day of my seventeenth birthday. It was one of the best days of my life. I rode that bike religiously for the next two weeks. I thought I was the coolest kid in school. Every day, waking up to ride the bike felt like Christmas morning.

At the time I was living with my dad and my bedroom was the front room of the house. I came home around 2 a.m., had sixth form the next day and had to be up at 6 a.m. to complete some coursework that was due in early. Usually I would wheel the bike around the back alley so it was out of sight of passers-by, but I was knackered and stupidly parked it right outside the front. The steering lock was on and my bedroom window open, with the bike parked so nearby I could have literally slept with my hand out the window resting on the handlebars.

My lovely dog Diesel was a pitbull who would bark hours before the postman came. Now despite living in South London and fully understanding the risk I was taking, I fell asleep a gambling man. Some lessons have to be learnt the hard way.

I woke up and the bike was gone.

I informed the police, but I wasn't going to sit around and wait. Knowing this was probably a spontaneous theft, I knew the chances of the bike still being somewhere close by would be quite high. So I withdrew the remaining £150 I had to my name and took Diesel around the area offering anyone the £150 reward if they could tell me where my bike was.

Nothing. I came home that night and remember watching a film where the main character lost his family, his house and everything else. It felt like the film was trying to teach me something. Money comes and goes. Having health, friends and family is all that truly matters.

The following days we continued the search, feeling less and less hopeful. I came home to a letter saying that my bike had been caught speeding down Acre Lane. I got gassed; I thought this was a lead. My dad sheepishly pointed out that the date the photograph on the letter had been taken. It was the day before my bike was stolen, which means it was me riding the bike, and me who was speeding. I had to pay the £80 fine, so I now had £70 left.

I wasn't going to spend my life feeling sorry for myself, so I started working at Miss P's BBQ flipping burgers in Brixton.

Two years later, I was at a modelling job in North London when I received a call: 'Have you been involved in a robbery?' I said, 'Shut up Jack or whoever this is, I'm at work, what is it?'

'This is the police, did you report a bike stolen?'

Police had found the bike behind a block in Streatham, about a fifteen-minute drive from my dad's house where it was originally taken. They said it was in good condition and that if we could pick it up within the hour they wouldn't charge the £250 impound fee.

Growing up my mum would sacrifice her weekends and allow me, my brother and his friends to lift up the seats of her Toyota Previa, chuck our bikes in the back and take them to joyride outside of London. Now, since I was on the other side of the city, I called my mum and begged her to do this for me, one last time.

Being a mother, she jumped in the car and picked up the bike immediately.

I don't get to ride it much any more as I don't really have the time, but I still have the bike to this day. The story of my Aprilia RS4 125 Alitalia edition is one of the most valuable lessons of my life. My mum always references one thing I said to her the night the bike was taken.

She says: *I'll never forget, when you told me the bike was stolen and I said how sorry I was that that had happened to you Hero, you replied, you know what Mum, I just hope whoever has my bike right now needs it more than I do.*

Now don't get me wrong. I was obviously happy to get the bike back. But I now understand that the lesson learnt was more valuable than the bike itself.

Don't Listen

BEN SHEPHARD

Broadcaster, journalist and friend

Someone once said, '*Find a job you love and you'll never work a day in your life!*' For twenty-plus years I would certainly count myself in that category.

However, it could have been very different.

About fifteen months into the early stages of my career one of the channel bosses I was working for, but whom I'd never met, called me into her office to explain in no uncertain terms that I wasn't going to be working there any longer. Not only was I not cut out for this sort of job, I never would be, and I should find a different career path to follow because, in her opinion, I would never make it in the world of TV and certainly not live television.

This TV controller had years of experience and influence, she was an expert, she had power. In her mind she had seen through me, my lack of talent and skill. What she saw, in her opinion, was not someone who could be a TV presenter; I just didn't have the potential.

As I think back to that day I can vividly recall it. The glass walls of her office, the febrile atmosphere, her big hair, my fear of confusion and devastation. It is no less striking a moment now than it was twenty years ago.

So why didn't I listen to her? Well, for two reasons.

Firstly, I wanted to prove her wrong. Really wrong. In a burning, feral, two-fingered type way.

Secondly, I remember thinking about the people who had given me my chance. The people who had seen my potential. The people who did think I had the ability, despite my lack of experience.

Their positivity and enthusiasm became my focus; theirs would be the opinions I would listen to and rely on. Through their support and my determination I was going to prove her wrong.

I learnt a valuable lesson that day: TV and life can be brutal. There will always be people in positions of power who, for whatever reason, don't believe in you, see your potential, skills or ability. The question is how you react to that feedback. Will it change you, alter your aspirations and bring you down? Or will it inspire you, drive you forward and fire you up?

Twenty years later I'm still not working a day in my life – because I found a job I loved, and it turns out, despite what some might think, I'm not that bad at it after all!!

I Am A Piano

JASPREET KAUR (BEHIND THE NETRA)

Poet, author, activist, educator

I am a piano
From the Italian origin of the word pianoforte,
Meaning soft but strong.

'It's ironic how much love you give out but you don't love
    yourself?'
I never found it ironic.
Not when writing poetry was putting all that love I couldn't
    give myself to good use.
But that all changed when I realised I love someone enough to
    want to love myself too.
Now I am a piano,
I am soft but strong.

But before that, I found myself with empty pens, notebooks
    filled with poems,
I tucked pieces of myself into my words.
I had enough pages to stitch them into wings,
Fly to the sun so I could see my tears evaporate into steam.
Until those tears covered my body like wax,
Now I had thick skin.
Now I am a piano,
I am soft but strong.

Soon I realised that everything beautiful doesn't have to have a
    consequence,
And maybe I just needed to be in darkness for a while so I
    could see the stars.
Now I am a piano,
I am soft but strong.

And even when I think about those times that my keys were
    pressed without my permission,
I actioned an escapement.
This is the mechanism in a piano that allows the hammer to
    escape after a string has been struck,
So leaving the string to vibrate.
Until I finally reached a frequency where I could play
    symphonies again,
Now I am in harmony.
Now I am a piano,
I am soft but strong.

Mummy's Boy & Daddy's Princess

RYAN ADAGIO WINCH

Father, director and friend

For Alyla-Marie Winch

Congratulations, you're a dad, the best day of your life,
well that's what they said but that's not what I felt inside.
You have ocean eyes so I hid my feelings with compulsive lies
and got ready for my biggest battle with compromise.

I was scared to be alone with you,
scared when I was holding you.
Scared to talk about the feelings I was going through
but day after day my bond grows with you
because everything and more is what I owe to you.

It was hard to know my role and find my feet as father.
I was battling depression and trying to find answers.
There's still a fine line between your tears and laughter
but every time you hurt I'll be here with a plaster

See I grew up around gangs, drugs, stabbing and firing.
I made it out now Hussain calls me inspiring.
My friend from nursery got murdered he can't father his son
so I got no excuses for the adult you become.

Because I'm gonna love and nurture, push you further.
Hold Mummy close because truth be told I don't deserve her
And you gave me purpose, a reason to get up.
When I wanted to give up your love made me better.

So innocent and pure, you deserve the world and more.
Terrible twos watching you push boundaries and explore.
Bumps and bruises, more stories to tell
and as you grow older you will always be my little girl

I'm a mummy's boy and you're daddy's princess,
You love football and finding insects.
Doing Daddy's makeup and climbing at the park
or climbing out your cot head first in the dark.

There's beauty in the struggle but we're finding our way.
Finding balance in providing and having time to play.
I cherish every moment when I'm watching you grow
because time flies by you're nearly three years old.

Times I wanted to give up it was you that got me through
so I'll give up on breathing before I give up on you.
The good, the bad, the ugly, the happy and sad.
The first word you muttered was da-da-Dadd.

Small Mercies

JEREMY VINE

Sometimes I think a near-death experience can be a really good thing.

As a result of an incident on my penny-farthing – I bought this enormous bicycle, designed in 1880, and did some kind of upside-down cartwheel over the handlebars when I hit a divot – I started to think about near-death experiences. Generally we never think about death because we just aren't programmed to. But sometimes we're confronted by it; we might have a relative die, or see a terrible event overseas, or, in my case, we might fall off a penny-farthing. Something terrible happens. No one wants the terrible thing, but what about the nearly-terrible, the narrow squeak? I've come to the view that one of the best things we have in life is when something terrible nearly happens.

Winston Churchill said, 'There is nothing in life quite so exhilarating as being shot at without result.' When I was a very young reporter I was fired on in Croatia and a bullet went so close to my head that you could hear the sound of it cut the air – you could actually see the needle move on the tape recorder as the bullet passed less than a foot away from my head. I always thought every day after that, I've got to think of this whole life experience as a bonus.

So where do you get your hope from when all seems terrible? The answer is, focus on what *didn't* happen. You didn't get blown up and you didn't fall off a cliff. Focus on your breath. In, out. That's hope. Bad things have happened, but you avoided the worst. That's what hope is – when the lightning singes but leaves you standing.

I've got two teenage daughters, and I'm very aware that they are under the impression that the planet has only got about forty years left – in fact one of them misheard a news item to that effect when she was a little girl. A newscaster said, 'If we carry on as we are, temperatures will be irreversibly changed within fifty years.' Anna, then aged nine, thought it meant the planet would be gone in fifty years. Without me knowing it, my nine-year-old daughter had worked out that she would only live to be fifty-nine and had written the rest of her life off.

I think my job as a father is to purvey hope. To say, 'Girls, it's not as bad as you think' – okay, maybe not that, because it is *quite* bad. How about, 'Girls, you're right, it's quite bad, but we can find a little bit of light here and there.' As Dad, I am the ray collector. I will always try to find a ray of light to brighten things up.

Now what they don't know, because I've never really told them, is that I've had periods of my life where I've been completely hopeless – which is why I think hope is so precious. When I feel little moments of hope, I want to preserve them. Somebody once said, 'If you take away a man's hope, you take away their life.' I often feel that I'm on a hamster wheel when I'm broadcasting and reporting, and that I'm just distracting myself from the bigger issues. But if I do stop, I have a primal desire to know we're all heading in the right direction. At the moment, for example, people say this country has gone to the dogs. They say it's not on its knees any more, it is flat on its face. I feel inclined to go with that – as a journalist I know I naturally focus relentlessly on the negative – but then I check myself. It's not healthy to be negative. Let's catch a ray of light.

If we look back a century, we were about to go into two world wars on the trot, and I hope it's not clutching at straws to say we don't (quite) have that at the moment. Instead we have medical advances, we've got incredible leaps forward in dealing with cancer and diseases – there's a lot to be hopeful about – but what we are very bad at, I think, is counting our blessings. So, I try to reflect that, even when everything has gone wrong, there are one or two things that you can be hopeful about.

So – the penny-farthing. One day I crashed. The early bicycle had a massive front wheel because penny-farthings didn't have chains or gears, so you had to fix the pedal to the wheel. The size of the front wheel stops your feet spinning round at high speed! I always wanted to ride one and I thought if I don't buy one now and learn, I never will.

My penny-farthing was delivered from China (don't ask me why they are making them again) and I went out riding it. It took me around a year to get good at it and after three years I was overconfident. I was cycling in my local area on this wildly large bike, which makes everybody stare and laugh and point at you. I had to get home quickly, and I took a shortcut across the grass, which is the one rule you're never supposed to break. You're sitting with your head nine feet in the air and if you stop suddenly you're going to go over the handlebars.

I hit a divot and, according to a bystander, my flying position looked like something out of the Olympics. I whizzed in a star shape across the air and fell to the ground, knocking myself out in the process. I went to A & E, and they did the full analysis on me – blood clots, brain scans, X-rays, MRI. They said I looked okay but needed to just be careful and keep a close eye on myself. I thought, 'I feel okay, but maybe I should go to a spinal specialist.'

I saw this private spinal specialist round the corner that I had to pay for, and he did a scan on my spine. I walked in to get the readout, and he had a picture of my spine on the screen, and I could see that it was broken in two! It snapped halfway down, and I couldn't even feel it! I turned to the doctor and said, 'Bloody hell!' in a state of shock and awe, to which he responded, 'Oh don't worry, that's not your spine, that's the guy we had this morning.'

I said, 'What's his name?' to which he responded, 'Richard.' So I said, 'Before you take his spine off the screen, could you tell me what happened to him?' The doctor responded that Richard had tripped on a brick. I thought, so I've gone nine foot off a penny-farthing, somersaulted through the air and knocked myself out and I'm fine, and this poor guy snapped his spine tripping on a brick? I thought, well, there is hope.

We have to be thankful every day if we wake up and stumble around, and we can look at the sun – we can see and we can think and feel – that there is hope. There is hope even in the slightest movement.

The Author

RYAN KEEN, DAN DARE AND HUSSAIN MANAWER

Artist, musician, friend and songwriter and record producer

The world doesn't get me
I don't expect it too
Everyone around me, presses my buttons
Then life comes and presses them too

You haven't got a choice Hussain
You keep going, my friends keep telling me

You can do it and it's knowing
Only you can set you free

But I fell in the gap
I'm mentally trapped
I'm running the taps
I'm not holding it back
I'm not good with the chat
But I know all my facts
And if they don't listen
Imma have to do it in rap

I'm breaking down as I pour my art
I don't speak too much coz I know they laugh
I just sat at home I just wrote my scars

If you wanna know, life took my heart
There's a reason why that I fell apart
My whole life became my art
That's the reason why I just give me half
Coz I get overwhelmed when I feel a spark

I swear to God I won't flop you
Straight in your face man, I got you
But you gotta do this man, you got too
What you got to live for? A lot too
When doubt comes in, you better chat back
Suicide yeah, you better back chat
And the pressure of life, we gotta hack that
We gotta do this, where's all my gang at?

I just wanna meet the author
Coz I don't understand the lines you wrote
I'm trying to cross the border
Ripping out the pages that I know
I feel it in my spine now
Feeling like the stories getting old
So I wanna meet the author
Coz I'm misreading what you wrote

And nothing ever moves but the pain in me
I'm trying to hold on to what it takes from me
But what works for you
Aint the same for me
And what helps you
Really wasn't made for me

I'm sensitive and I'm paranoid
I'm always in my feelings
I overthink on overthinking
Can't you see that your boy needs healing?

And the lead character no I aint forgot
I can't turn the page, coz I lost the plot
Deep deep down yeah I might be lost
And you'd be here, if your soul was robbed
I just hold on tight to the hope I got
Each episode I fight my clock
I don't say goodbye to the things I drop
Coz when I meet my author I'm going to take my shot

I just wanna meet the author
Coz I don't understand the lines you wrote
I'm trying to cross the border
Ripping out the pages that I know
I feel it in my spine now
Feeling like the stories getting old
So I wanna meet the author
Coz I'm misreading what you wrote

Not every story is told
Some are never written
Go inside yourself
And make sure your author listens

I just wanna meet the author
Coz I don't understand the lines you wrote
I'm trying to cross the border
Ripping out the pages that I know

I feel it in my spine now
Feeling like the stories getting old
So I wanna meet the author
Coz I'm misreading what you wrote

I Typed 'Hope' In My Notes

JORDAN STEPHENS

Artist

Within a society that magics margins off our misery. That proliferates pity for profit. One of, if not the greatest freedom is the death of our despair. May the sun control us. Not the sunken trollings of those who lack flair. May the rain guide us. And may we remain vibrant in the wake of internalised tears and acidic attitudes. May we wake in the morning to the wake and mournings of rotten frames we never hung.

They need us to despair at the sight of ourselves in the hope that we don't look behind the mirror, and find glass ideals that need no more than the hammers we were born with. We will smash them. We'll make art not content till our hearts are content. You pray for more panic but our laws are organic. And when the time comes. When we realise that nothing external can define us. When we realise that the beliefs you sell us exist only within our own clouded fantasies.

We'll change our minds. And you better hope you were kind. Because we're fucking wicked.

The Need To Not Quit

GREG TARZAN DAVIS

Father, actor, friend, creative, artist

Being the smallest, slowest, least athletic on a team of very talented individuals is the ideal situation for a person to pack their bags and throw in the towel. It's hard to think you would even have a chance to participate in the live game under the big bright lights on Friday night in front of a packed crowd when you just don't fit the criteria as your peers are going to battle alongside you.

Well, that's how I felt starting out playing high school football. I was one of the slowest, smallest individuals on our team of D1/D2 athletes and it seemed as though I would never see the field during my high school career.

Many times, I wanted to quit simply out of frustration of not getting the chance I thought I deserved to show the coaching staff the talent I had within me. Realistically a part of me knew I wasn't at the level to compete with these groups of boys, but I was in denial. There was a point during my journey in high school playing football in my sophomore year, I was faced with the choice to either keep complaining about the lack of field time, or do something about it.

Looking back on my past experiences where I seemed to not have any success, I reverted to what I knew how to do best and that is put in the work. I understood at some point with constant repetition, a person can get better at whatever it is they consistently do. So that's what I did. Every morning I was the first one to show up to school in the weight room working out, after practice the last one to leave the field working on conditioning, footwork, speed, etc. It was a grind of a process, and halfway through my sophomore year in high school when there seemed to be no improvements in my physical status or any major leaps in my ability, nor was my play time increasing, I faced a moment of 'Why am I even wasting my time doing this?'

At that moment, I felt the strong urge to just quit and give up. Until I randomly came across a quote that read, 'Nothing you want in life comes easy.' What I wanted was to get better, what I wanted was to get on that football field and play, what I NEEDED was to not quit, and so I didn't. For the entirety of my tenth-grade year, I put my head down and put in the work with no results coming from the coaches putting me in the game, but results in myself.

I began to get bigger, and faster, understand the game more. I felt like a different person and by the time my junior year came I WAS a different person and everyone began taking note of it. We had had two talented players in my position already who were ahead of me, so I knew it would be work to outdo them and get some playing time, but I was up for the challenge. What I set out to do was to become great at the things that they weren't so good at; in that case I could see the field in certain situations because I would have been the better man in that position. Guess what? The plan worked and I slowly became integrated in the mix of plays and during games my number was being called to play. To shorten this story up, by my senior year in high school I had managed to weave my way into the starting line-up amongst the other talented guys and touch the field every game, impacting it the best way I could.

I share this story with you today to say, everything seems impossible at first glance, but with consistent work put in and a desire to achieve that thing you NEED, not want but NEED, it will become possible.

Oh yeah, And You Don't Get Tired, because You Can't Get Tired!!

A Chameleon's Skin

EMMA HEDILE AL-MUÑSHI

Writer and friend

When you ask me, how are you? I'm going to tell you, I'm not doing so great.

Imagine that. A bit of honesty. The kind that instantly makes people blanch. A revelation that puts you in a true place of vulnerability.

What if you think I'm crazy? What if my answer makes you uncomfortable? Or even worse, I'm just over-sensitive?

But you've asked me now. And I'm going to be brave and tell you exactly what's going on in this mental cloud of mine.

I'm struggling with the skin I'm in. On every level.

I used to marvel at the fact that I was a bit of a chameleon really. I'd jump from group to group and use my extroversion to make sure you never saw my flaws. And trust me, there are lots of them. But it's getting harder to be that shape-shifter.

My brain isn't quite as sharp as it used to be. The months of lack of sleep has caused those awkward bits of me to poke through. A stretching of self-beliefs manifesting in a host of unhelpful ways.

I must have dreamed the same nightmare four out of seven nights last week – showcasing a multitude of ways you can get fired from a job for just being yourself. And that's common for me when I'm feeling down. I call it my anxiety dream. I suppose some life experiences really do leave a mark.

Like, I didn't know how to adjust to my new post-partum body, holding back tears whenever I looked in the mirror. The one with the new lumps and bumps and the big old scar. The same scar that brought my beautiful child into this world also causes me anxiety. The infection that took hold made me feel like my body had failed me. I couldn't walk. I couldn't lift my son. And when I told them something wasn't right, I was brushed off. Now, I struggle to look at pictures of myself from back then. I'm fearful of growing my family.

Meanwhile, I still can't work out who I am meant to be. A mum, yes. Wholeheartedly so. But also, someone with a lot of baggage; a struggling writer; a neurotic woman who cares too much about what people think of her. How can all these things coexist?

Sometimes, in the dead of night, I don't feel like I'm enough. Enough of a human, enough of a mother, enough of a wife. Yet, I feel myself growing more and more selfish. Perhaps, I'm just going through the process of putting boundaries in place. The same ones that will save my brain from melting and my emotions from exploding. Protection, to ensure I am strong enough to always keep my family safe.

A carefully constructed facade of who I thought I was began to crumble away with each unfollow. With every cold shoulder. With every lost connection, a part of myself broke away and added to a feeling of failure. I'd become irrelevant.

These thoughts have been festering for some time now. But deep down, I know they're at odds with what I know to be the truth about myself.

So now it's my turn to ask myself something. What is my truth?

I'm a bit chaotic, but I enjoy life. I've gone through some really crappy experiences, but haven't we all? My son means the world to me and my body was his home for nine months. He's brought a new sense of purpose to this life and, every day, I can't wait to wake up and see the smile on his face. The pain and sickness my body went through was worth it.

No one else but me can judge me for my decisions. And any form of character assassination on their part shows more of their insecurities than my own. I am enough because I say I'm enough. I am fortunate enough to have what feels like an endless love. My husband has supported me through thick and thin. He's seen the ugly and the downright brutal, and he still married me – twice, I might add.

I needed the rotten parts and appendages to dissolve away. Remove themselves from my universe so that I could start fresh. Become a happier version of me. A new ecosystem where both new and old dreams can flourish.

You've had a bit of an insight into the chaos of my brain there. And all because you dared to ask me how I was. All these words are just me coming to terms with the fact that I'm human. And we all go through similar moments of self-doubt. These harsh thoughts aren't true though and I don't need to be a chameleon. I just need to be myself. Had you not asked if I was okay, I wouldn't have been able to piece myself back together.

Checking in on me gave me hope. Reminded me that it's okay not to be okay sometimes.

So. Ask me again if I'm okay. I'll tell you I'm doing much better, thank you so much for asking.

I Won't Be Beaten

GIAN POWER

CEO and entrepreneur

On 30 May 2015 I was about to receive news that would change my life forever. As a then 23-year-old I had always considered myself 'resilient', being able to manage the challenges that life threw my way, but I wasn't ready for this one.

Until that date, I'd had a happy childhood. I'd grown up with loving parents, my father a British Indian entrepreneur and my mother who's dedicated her life to helping others in the community. In the summer of 2014 I graduated from university and it was smiles all round as I headed to London to start my career with Big Four accounting firm PwC – not knowing at the time just how important the power of a smile was going to be. Because nine months later, my life changed forever.

On a crisp morning in May of 2015, my father took a flight overseas on a business trip and, as the days passed by, it seemed that nobody had heard from him. As the worry started to escalate, panic set in. Three weeks of being missing and three weeks of me doing all I could to find him all came to a head that morning. I found out that my father had been murdered.

I will never forget the day. The day that shook my world, but it was the day I had to grow up, step up and play the role of my dad to myself and to others in the family. The emotional toll was huge, and the challenges continued to hit me. Some time later I repatriated my father's body to the UK – only to be told it was not his body. Now I find myself with someone else's body in the UK, yet someone had confessed to my father's murder in India – oh and at this point things were about to take a further turn.

In the following years, I would find myself in endless court battles, people I thought were close to me began taking all my father's assets and I lost my family home, my car and even most of my childhood belongings. It was painful but I had to keep going. It was the only way.

I won't be beaten. I refuse to be beaten. Each time I was knocked down, I was determined to rise again. Above all, I knew that all these difficult days were making and shaping the person I needed to be. Throughout everything I always prioritised my wellbeing. When fighting in courts, dealing with international police, the media and more, I had to bring my A game. I knew there was only one way to do that. Look after my mental health.

Since the day I received the news about my father, I had known that the success of justice was directly linked to how well I could look after my mind. Resilience is not about a 'keep going mentality' – resilience is about knowing how to recover, when you need to recover to then perform at your best. It's something I continue to take very seriously and that allows me to keep going because I will never be beaten.

Life throws its challenges at us and I've learnt that the comfort zone is a lovely place but nothing grows there. Each time we are forced into difficult situations, they feel intense, heavy and never-ending. I promise you to keep hope, keep smiling and know that one day, *the future you is going to be so proud.*

Are there days when things feel too much? Yes. But let it out, feel your emotions and then look at yourself in the mirror. Look at how far you have come and learn to see the beautiful side of everything on this Earth.

Remember – you are unique, you are special, and you have a gift. That gift might be shaped by difficult times and struggles in your life, but lean into it, learn from it and continue to smile. Yes, at times it is hard, but I learnt that people could take my father, take all my possessions, but nobody will ever take my smile.

So, smile with pride, smile with honour. For your smile will help so many continue to fight on each day. Never ever give up.

When Life Gives You Lemons

BRADY CAMPBELL

Student and friend

When I was just six years old, I had this great idea to do a lemonade stand for my mom. My dad loved the idea and told me that we could do it in secret to surprise her when she came back from a trip she was on. I was so excited about it, and I wanted to use the money I made to take my mom out on a date. But things didn't go as planned.

My dad got sick and was diagnosed with stage 4 colon cancer. We had to delay our lemonade stand until later, hoping he would get better. But he got sicker and sicker, and eventually he found out he was going to pass away. Despite his condition, he helped me make the signs for the lemonade stand and told me, 'Do the lemonade stand even if I pass away. Take your mom on a nice dinner and take care of her.'

The day after my dad died, my grandma and aunt helped me set up the lemonade stand to surprise my mom. It was hard to keep going without my dad by my side, but I knew I had to do it for him. My first customer was a police officer, and he gave me $20 for just two glasses of lemonade. It was my lucky $20. He called other police officers and firefighters, and soon the whole community came to buy lemonade..

I got to ride in a police car and even go to the top of the ladder on a fire truck. It was an amazing day, and I raised $241. But it didn't stop there. The news station heard about it, and we got to go to New York City and went on *Good Morning*

176

America. People from all over the world donated to my lemonade stand, and we raised over $50,000.

My mom and I went on many dates after that, and we even decided to start a fund at the University of Colorado Anschutz, where my dad was treated. We donated the lemonade stand funds there to the palliative care team for grief and bereavement support. It was my dad's wish to support them, and we were happy to help others just like they helped us.

I miss my dad a lot, but I know he would be proud of what we've done. Even when things are tough, we should never give up on our dreams. My dad taught me that, and I will always remember his words: 'Take your mom on a nice dinner and take care of her.'

I am now ten years old. When I think back on this story I have some advice to share with others going through tough situations. Don't be afraid to ask for help, allow those people to help you, and take things one small step at a time.

We Are Being Completely Erased From Society
ANONYMOUS

It was a typical Thursday on 22 December 2022 as I left the Afghanaid office for the weekend. I never thought however that it could be my last day working in the office, as the ban on women working in NGOs was announced just two days later.

In December, Afghanaid had just signed at least three new contracts for delivering humanitarian assistance projects over the winter. This winter was particularly harsh, so these new projects were going to be a massive help for the people in our working areas. It was a challenging year for me personally, but I was happy with my performance at work as the year was ending.

I have been the main income earner for my family for the past year after everyone else lost their income sources due to the growing economic decline in Afghanistan. But my job has been more than just a livelihood for me. Working has been a way for me to cope with all the stress I feel because of the dire situation of women's rights in my country. I am sure it has been the same for my other female colleagues as well.

I found out about the new decree because my friend texted me about it and sent a copy of the letter signed by the Ministry of Economy. I was shocked because it came out of nowhere. When the Taliban took over Afghanistan, I expected them to announce such a ban at that time. But a year and a half later, it is difficult to understand the real motivations and intentions behind the ban. But I was disappointed and disheartened more than anything else.

All human beings should have the right to work and earn an income. NGOs have always been in a unique position where women have had the opportunity to grow professionally and gain financial independence, regardless of all the barriers created by different regimes. And in return these women have been instrumental in enabling NGOs to reach women and girls across the country. Therefore, by banning NGOs from employing women, many avenues for improving women's living conditions in Afghanistan will be closed.

The public sphere for women in Afghanistan was already extremely limited but, after the two recent decrees that deprive women of their basic rights to get an education and to work, I see that we are being completely erased from society.

The humanitarian crisis in Afghanistan is very real, and this ban is significantly disrupting the ability of aid organisations to deliver assistance to the most vulnerable population, who are women and girls. It clearly violates humanitarian principles and leaves an even larger number of people with no food and shelter amidst one of the harshest winters in the country. I am infuriated and disheartened that the Taliban are turning a blind eye to the immense suffering Afghan people are going through.

Every day on my way to the office, I would see a lot of daily wage labourers standing in the streets from very early in the morning waiting for someone to ask them to work. Many of my relatives who lost their jobs now completely rely on remittance. These were all middle class families before the Taliban takeover. Those who graduated from university haven't been able to find a job. The salaries of most government employees were cut by 50 per cent. Those who are retired have not gotten their pensions at all since the Taliban takeover. The private sector has largely collapsed as on most job portals the only job advertisements are those from the NGOs. In the last few weeks, different news channels reported that around 160 people, most of whom were women and children, have died in different parts of the country because of the freezing cold weather. I am sure that in reality, the actual numbers will be much more than that.

I still cannot believe that women are now told simply not to exist, while just a few years ago women's rights and girls' education were noted amongst the biggest achievements of the international community's presence in Afghanistan. Therefore, now I implore the donor countries and the international community to find ways of reversing this ban. I believe that they owe this to the Afghan people.

I definitely refuse to lose hope, but unfortunately right now it doesn't seem like a major breakthrough will happen any time soon.

Afghanaid is a British humanitarian and development organisation that has worked with and for Afghans for forty years. They build basic services, improve livelihoods, strengthen the rights of women and children, help communities protect themselves against natural disasters and adapt to climate change, and respond to humanitarian emergencies.

In response to this ban, Afghanaid – alongside various delegations, the UN agencies and other NGOs – has been engaging with the de facto authorities to advocate for a full reversal of the decree. Alongside this, and thanks to Afghanaid's Afghan-majority team, community-led approach and longstanding presence in the remote, rural areas they serve, they have been able to devise localised solutions across their areas of work that enable them to continue to reach women directly while protecting and maintaining the meaningful inclusion of female staff.

For more information about their work and how they continue to deliver life-saving and life-changing assistance under the Taliban regime, please visit www.afghanaid.org.uk.

Promise Me

CHIDERA EGGERUE AKA THE SLUMFLOWER

Author

Promise me you won't give up on yourself
Even when it feels like you need too much help
Promise me you will let them see your light
Even when standing tall feels like a fight
Promise me you'll always choose yourself
Even when the voice swears you need someone else
Promise me you won't believe your anxiety
Even when its lie looks like reality
Promise me you won't give up on yourself
There's a blessing behind every card you've been dealt.

Emotionally Fragile

HUSSAIN MANAWER

I said goodbye to my life
The day I said hello to you in the sky
I've got no shame to say that I cry
Everytime, I can't rhyme, I feel another angel and come fly by
My shoes are worn
My foot prints carry the soul of my stride

Crew on board it's your captain speaking
The deep end, we've hit turbulence
The cycle tries repeating
Life in the manner is merciless
I need you all to remain seated
Midlife - can't be purposeless
The main priority should be healing
Before the pain becomes permanent

I got passion and pain really fighting
everything is emotive
All these issues underlying
One little triggers explosive
I get overwhelmed I know what to do
I gotta take my life in doses
Flash in the dark it hits it spikes at lightening I can't sit and
wait for diagnosis

I'm letting it go, I'm letting it be, i'm done with all the
suppressing
If i don't trust my gut at this stage, to my bloodline that is
offensive
I gotta protect my spirit so you can say I'm defensive
I've been drawn out, and i've been overdrawn
distractions are really expensive

I've got bad habits and that's counterproductive
All I can hear are the sounds of the tractor
It's eruptive, I'm self destructive
Spirit and soul are feeling the fracture
In an episode now it's not constructive
My heart really needs an adapter

Behavior patterns that are all disruptive
Let's go deeper into the chapter

I'm swinging on a pendulum
Between the worlds and it's evident
From Mangla Dam to Beverly Hills
I'm Your local global resident

With Mum saving elephants
Fighting against the prejudice
There's pain in my face and it's evidence
Feel blessings that are still so heaven sent

I'm climbing I can't Ever-rest
Feel it in every sentiment   —
Our hurt is really delicate
We need discipline in our regiments

Break through all of these measurements
And the temperature of the temperament
Tells me, our pain and stories, life and glory
Is really relevant

I'm the happiest that I've ever been
With the least i've ever had
I'm traveling the world i'm a hunchback
But lets cutback to get playback
Coz they still wanna check my rucksack
I got a pen and the pad in my backpack
But i can't react to the back chat
So I write to you all with straight facts

I treat my life like a cypher
If its goes deep i'm a diver
If they wanna attack im a striker
I speak to the facts and I get to the point
There's not much left to decipher
They say the jab can take you around the world
Hence why I weren't keen on the phiza

I've spent too long in the pit tops
I'm center mid for when it kicks off
Im in Lahore, Pakistan with the big crops
For the pain in my heart when the ink drops
walkside, Dover, cliff tops,
more sticks and stones for my slingshot
LA Melrose thrift shops
This Space boy was ready for the lift off!

When it's down in the manner and they've all got a dagger, it
gets lonely when your so lo

When you put it in the grammar, but they do it for the glamor
there's places that we can't go no

When you're climbing up the ladder and they shoot another
banger and death is coming in slow mo

The shires moving madder, coz theres all getting badder and if
you enter the ring, you better Fro-do

The originals in the instruments
When it's lyrical I get meticulous
At the pinnacle there's predicaments
There unforgivable with their wickedness
It's divisible and it's hideous
But that's typical for maliciousness
Miracles and it's ridiculous
My syllables are in the syllabus

I had to re-start my engine
Off of the grid
I had to put it this all into a book,
Coz I wanted to quit
I had to open my heart
And blow off the lid

But the Pen in my hand never let go the grip

Hopefully I lock it i'm agile,
Socially I'm off it i'm tactile

Locally I'm on it ran miles
Emotionally you clocked it i'm fragile

PART FOUR

Help

GREG WILLIAMS
ROGER STREAKO KING TUTU
JOEL ROBISON
HOLLY-MARIE CATO
DHILLAN B
FADY ELSAYED
NATASHA ALI
KIERON BOOTHE
KIRSTY LATOYA
HUSSAIN MANAWER
GOODY FROM LEEDS
STEEL BANGLEZ
LUCREZIA MILLARINI
BASHIR 'DOUBLE S' BAZANYE
OBAIDULLAH
QAMAR JABARKHYL

Comfortingly Confronting – A Conversation
GREG WILLIAMS AND HUSSAIN MANAWER

An open and honest conversation with photographer
Greg Williams and Hussain Manawer

HUSSAIN: When we met, probably for the second or third time, we properly connected in the Chateau Marmont.

GREG: Probably was second time yeah.

HUSSAIN: I think so yeah, because I didn't have your number.

GREG: Yeah, we talked through instagram.

HUSSAIN: Yeah, we met and then we spoke.

GREG: I feel like I've known you forever, so it's special.

HUSSAIN: I know, I know, it does, you were very generous with your love and your kindness and then I left and drove back to the Joshua Tree and was awake all night, and was thinking I want to chat to him again. Then I came back the next day to speak to you again.

GREG: Yeah.

HUSSAIN: And then I was like, umming and ahhing, and then I asked you if you would help me. And erm, and probably yeah the first and only person I've ever really said that to . . .

GREG: Okay, why do you think that was?

HUSSAIN: I don't know, I think I felt safe, loved and also challenged in a confronting but yet what's the word . . .

GREG: Comfortingly confronting?

HUSSAIN: Yeah, yeah that's it, in a confronting way.

GREG: Comfortingly confronting, that's quite nice.

HUSSAIN: Yeah and that's really rare man, and so I was really glad we had that conversation.

GREG: Okay, good.

HUSSAIN: And I didn't feel less of a man for asking for help, if anything I felt more of.

GREG: Yeah, it's a manly thing to do, there's nothing manly about digging a hole and sitting in it and hoping the situation improves without doing anything about it yourself. So asking for help is a step towards a better place. What are we if we can't ask for help?

If you can ask for help when you need it, what makes you so special that you don't need help? Everyone needs help. Why would you be so arrogant to think that it would be wrong to ask for help?

HUSSAIN: I think a lot of the time I was thinking I am too much . . . too intense.

GREG: But you are too two tents, you are a wigwam and a teepee.

HUSSAIN: Wait, what does that mean?

GREG: A wigwam.

HUSSAIN: What's that?

GREG: It's a tent.

HUSSAIN: Yeah.

GREG: And a teepee is also a tent.

HUSSAIN: Yeah.

GREG: So you're two tents.

HUSSAIN: Is that a good thing? Is that a bad thing, I don't understand.

GREG LAUGHS

GREG: What, being two tents?

HUSSAIN: *LAUGHS*
Ohh intense, that went over my head.

GREG: Yeah I know man, you gotta speed up round here
You're a wigwam and a teepee, you're two tents.
But na, it's great how tense you are, you're passionate and
you are fucking fantastic.

HUSSAIN: Thank you.

GREG: You are super talented.

HUSSAIN: Thank you. As are you. I learn so much from you,
I'm always learning so much from you.
I really just wanted to start the chapter of this book
by letting people know that at thirty years old I was
asking for help. And I thank you for allowing me the
space to do that and ever since then moving forward as
well.

GREG: Now you are trying to get back out of moving to Los
Angeles.

HUSSAIN: No I'm not.

GREG LAUGHS

HUSSAIN: I was telling my mate I was going to see you today
and he said I'll be in America tomorrow.

GREG: *LAUGHS*
Ah, did he?

HUSSAIN: Yeah, he knows I'll be in America tomorrow, but there's another thing you said to me on the last trip in America, you said to me, 'I'm not in Kansas any more.'

GREG: Yeah.

HUSSAIN: I think you can see I'm a fish out of water in a lot of these places and spaces with all these different faces and I'm just trying to navigate accordingly in the most authentic way. Which is hard innit?

GREG: Yeah that's what we gotta do, that's what people respond to as well.

My whole business is based around authenticity, and how to capture people authentically and how to show an authentic side to someone in an industry that in itself is a facade.

So authentically, if you look at the greatest artists, photographers, poets, film-makers, the greatest writers, you inherently believe what you are seeing, hearing, reading, watching and listening to. It's all about authenticity. And not enough people strive for that. And you are deeply authentic. You wear your heart on your sleeve to such an extent and you mix that with real talent. So it's really exciting. You are an exciting person to help. I get asked to help lots of people but you can't help everyone, you don't serve anyone by helping everyone.

I know I can't do it, it takes too much of my brain, it costs too much. You can't help too many people. So you have to choose who you help.

HUSSAIN: Well, I'm glad it's me!

GREG: Me too.

HUSSAIN: I think this is a great way to start the chapter, and yeah thank you. I am still trying to find the correct term for you in my life, I don't think mentor does it justice.

GREG: What about mental?

BOTH LAUGH AND HUG

£500

GREG WILLIAMS

Photographer and friend

Early in my career I started quite well. I was nineteen and I
went off and did my second ever assignment. My first job I
ever did was photographing the war in Burma, I was smuggled
into Burma with a mate, and my second job was photographing
the terrible drought that was hitting southern Africa on the
borders of Zimbabwe and Mozambique. And when I came
back the photos I took won me Young Photographer of the Year
and it was for everyone under the age of thirty and I was
nineteen. I was very young to win it.

I was on a high and my family were all excited about it and
people who were into photography had an eye I suppose on
me, and then nothing really happened. And the truth is I
hadn't learnt enough technically, so technically I wasn't that
strong. Then I went off and started doing jobs that slowly
started whittling away at my confidence. I kept talking about
wanting to be a photojournalist but really I was standing
outside premieres and parties and was trying to do stories but
they weren't big or important enough. So this great start really
felt like it was fizzling out.

By the time I was twenty-two/twenty-three, I was on a bit of
a low. I had a friend who gave me a kick up the ass; he said,
'What the hell are you doing? You started with all this promise
and we all got really excited about you and now you're sitting
round not really doing it, it's underwhelming'. He said if I

wanted to be a photojournalist I should be in Chechnya right now. It was the very beginning of the war in Grozny in 1995 when Russia was attacking the Chechens and it was the big story. It was a hard news story and it would have been a real testing ground.

Honestly, I was petrified and not very motivated, and we talked and the next day there's a knock on the door and it's 6.45 in the morning and I'm thinking, 'who's that?' and he's banging on the door and it's my mate and he's got this envelope full of cash, with around £500–£600 in it, and he says 'I'm in a hurry, I don't have time, but here's some money so go to Chechnya. I don't want it back. But one day when you can afford to, pass it on to someone else.'

And that act of kindness helped restart my photography career. And I've passed it on several times since.

Mountain To Climb

ROGER STREAKO KING TUTU

Music artist

In life, there comes a time
When we must choose a path to climb
And though it may be steep and long
We know we must be brave and strong

You're facing challenges, it's true
But you have dreams that you pursue
A life of music, passion, joy
A journey that you can't avoid

It's natural to feel scared or lost
To wonder what will be the cost
But don't forget the strength you hold
The power of your heart, so bold

So take a breath, and take a step
And don't give up, don't you forget
That you are worthy, you are strong
You'll find your way, where you belong

Your music is your heart and soul
Your passion, your ultimate goal
So keep on climbing, keep on striving
And know that you are truly thriving.

Threading A Needle Through My Imagination
JOEL ROBISON

Artist, friend, creative

There I was, storm clouds rolling through the mountains in front of me and storm clouds rolling through the thoughts inside me. Tall grass waving and brushing against my skin. I stood feeling the electricity in the air and the charge of every atom, every fibre of myself burning through my body. I was a house on fire, a tree chopped down, a version of myself that I didn't recognise, and I couldn't find a way out. I could run, if I really wanted to.

I thought about quitting. I thought about packing a bag and going away where nobody would find me. I thought about jumping, about hiding, about leaving the world that didn't feel like it cared that much about me any more. But there was a break in the clouds. A golden glow from the setting sun that forced its way through, burning back the grey and shining great golden beams of light right into my face. I raised the camera and took the photo, a souvenir of this moment that stopped me in my tracks. An image of hope in the midst of a thick and heavy sky.

My mind has always been the thing that attacks me but also the thing that saves me. A two-sided coin that is in constant imbalance and I can never predict when the coin toss happens and I'm hit with the side I'm not prepared for. But when I'm feeling those heavy thoughts, the cloudy ones with whispers of self-doubt or worries about what others may think of me, I know that the other side of the coin holds all the answers to get me through it. I know that I can open the map inside my mind and navigate to a world where daydreams will unfold before me and paint a visual that explains much more than vowels and consonants could ever do. I can lift a camera to my eye, put my photos into a computer and piece together a puzzle that both builds up an image that lays out everything I'm feeling and takes those feelings away at the same time. Each piece taken from one side of my mind and put back into another, a constant game of balance within me. Taking down one house to build another.

I remember sitting once, a decade ago, my face hovering inches away from the computer screen staring back at a man I didn't know. It was me, just ten years after the last time I'd really noticed who I was. I'd avoided mirrors, I'd avoided windows, photos, I was avoiding myself. I was afraid of seeing whoever it was that was living my life. I sat in a quiet room and let my face take up the screen. I saw a wrinkle under my eye, a freckle on my nose, I saw every worry and every negative thought scattered through blue eyes looking back at me. I stared at myself so long that I couldn't tell which side was me, until I realised that both sides were. The one on the screen who was telling my story, and the one sitting and feeling tears pool and his heart thumping.

Creating photos, building a story using the bricks that I throw at myself, has been my way out, my way through. All the times I wanted to quit, to quit life, to quit being an artist, to quit being myself, have been stopped by taking those sharp pieces that feel like broken glass and putting them back together into a visual that explains it all to myself. It's a mosaic of my anxiety, of my worries, my fears, my weighed-down thoughts. And in the process it's connected me with others too, people I know and people I'll never know. People who understand because their stories are made from the same glass and bricks, and some people who have never felt the world crumble beneath them. It makes each of us a little more human, even through pixels on a screen.

I still get lost. Never in the city, or in the woods, never when there is a map or a path to guide me out. I get lost in my mind where nothing leads to a waypoint. But when I'm lost, I can pull out my camera, I can close my eyes and ask myself to tell someone else what it looks like right now. I can thread a needle with my imagination and sew together all the different scraps of what I'm feeling and present an image that explains it all with no words at all. A tiny box with a mirror, a computer with a mouse, and a moment to let my mind wander into the side that sees the hope and beauty in the world is all it takes for me to want to keep going. To continue to be a storyteller, to continue to share with others and hope that they see that their story, their ideas, their art, their lives are worth sharing too.

Soloraves, A Raincoat And A Dog Named Sparta

HOLLY-MARIE CATO

Photographer and director

I'm what is called a high-functioning depressive. I will fly 3,000 miles on very little sleep, turn up on time and do my job while being the most entertaining person in the room. I'll be attentive, I'll listen to your problems and leave you on a high, all while my own joy receptors are at a minimum. I'll smile, I'll laugh, I'm likeable. But at times when the grip of depression feels its strongest, I barely remember what it feels like to be happy. Surrounded in a room full of people, I'm masking hard and underneath it all feeling empty.

When left too long to my own devices, a heavy-handed vignette, like a cloud circling the edges of my vision, caves in and my world, like a never-ending whole, becomes consumed with just one weighty feeling: despair. It's often then that I'll retreat to the comfort of my bed, totally oblivious to time or a shower, until I am summoned, most likely by some job opportunity, a birthday or a loved one's emergency, and it's up and out to perform again. There's other times, though, when this thick black cloud is punctured by friends who have noticed I've been quiet and absent. Who turn up uninvited with fresh flowers and mangos or light up my phone with calls and texts to help guide me back to myself again.

Even if I fail to show it, I'm so grateful to those friends and for each and every mirror they've held up, affirming who they know me to be and all the value my life carries when I lose my way. One of those friends is Hussain, who's listened to me at my worst and guided me back.

In this space of learning how to navigate seasons of depression I've compiled a list of things that have helped me. This is not a failsafe list of things that will save you. This is an account of the things that have punctured the void for me and allowed light in.

1. **Running** – I don't look like your traditional runner, I'm not fast, I'm not slim and my breathing lacks technique, but running found me when I needed it the most. And what I found was, if I could make my body move, to jog a certain distance or a length of time, then I could face anything else the day could throw at me, because the hardest work was done. I set a goal and proved I could do it and in a way it made me believe in myself. Beyond more than just where my body could carry me, I believed I was capable of finding happiness in my future. It was a therapy of sorts and it wasn't easy. There were many tears shed between KMs and dirt paths and so much fulfilment found there too. Hussain has been my accountability partner numerous times with running and I've been his. We've swapped sweaty selfies for years to prove we moved that day and hopefully felt better for it.

2. **Fasting** – now consult your doctors and nutritionist because I'm not a specialist, but fasting helped me when I felt at my very worst. I remember being three days into a ten-day fast with friends, who as Christians were engaging in the act of fasting and praying as part of our faith walk and me very much participating out of some self-inflicted peer pressure and thinking this was a monumental waste of time. Yet somewhere between days

five and seven a weight was lifted. The numbness and despondency was over and I could feel again and the feeling felt mostly like joy.

3. **A raincoat** – running is great but let's be real, there are many times when getting out of bed, let alone running, feels too hard. So let's go for a walk. Once you have made that decision DO IT. Don't even let wet weather stop you from getting fresh air and being outside. Own a raincoat. There's been many a time I've let rain meet the tears on my face as I battle demons in a walk through the park. Just move your legs, take deep breaths and acknowledge you are alive.

4. **A pet (preferably a dog)** – there's a reason why dogs are called a (wo)man's best friend. Dogs love us unconditionally. I used to take care of my uncle's dog, Sparta, who I've had on and off since she was a puppy. Unfortunately I travel too much to keep her permanently, but when I was in town I'd have Sparta for days or even weeks at a time. She gave me love and affection and forced me into a routine. I became responsible for feeding, walking and playing with this creature and ultimately looking after myself a bit better too.

5. **Boxing** – because nothing feels better than punching something hard when you are down. Just make sure it's a bag, instructor or sparring partner and not someone who hasn't agreed to physical contact.

6. **A basic-ass to-do list** – people told me for years, 'write a list, put it on paper!' and I resisted. Now, three decades into life, I can confirm they work. But when I am going through *IT* (and by *IT* I mean depression) a list can look a little different. Often these lists will look a lot simpler yet require the same amount of effort to achieve.

IT lists often look like this:
- Get out of bed
- Drink some water & take your vitamins
- Shower
- Skincare
- Answer three emails
- Eat fruit
- Go for a walk today
- Eat dinner

7. **A playlist of your favourite songs** – music is powerful, but now is not the time for your list of sad melancholic breakup songs, we specifically want to play music that get you up and shaking your hips. I challenge you to a solo boogie – nothing feels more euphoric than a three-minute rave in the privacy of your home!

8. **Ask for help** – you are not fine and that's okay. Let those you trust know how you're doing. Good friendships aren't a substitute for seeking professional help – most of us will need both. But if you, like me, are the visibly strong one in your community, your people might not instantly understand what you are going through and you may need to have grace for them. You may also need to reassess those relationships. I hope that you are able to communicate your needs; in time that support system will be stronger for it.

I Threw It On A T-Shirt

DHILLAN B

CEO of Ratchet Clothing

Hi, so I've never thought, nor did I ever think I was ever gonna be writing my success story in a book for other people to read, but here we are. I don't really know properly how I got here myself but f*** it, and welcome to the journey of being an Asian boy in a kinda strict home and breaking the rules to becoming the UK's largest independent streetwear brand.

It all kinda started off when I was sixteen and I left school with zero qualifications. I knew that I didn't really need to try hard in school because in the Asian community you basically go to work for your parents, especially if you're a male, so a little info on my family: I mean my grandad immigrated into the UK in the sixties and stereotypically started a taxi firm and a cornershop business.

Then he made enough money to bring his wife and three sons over to the UK. My dad was the firstborn child in the UK and ever since that day we've always stuck together as a family – and when I say stuck together I mean we live together forever and we are currently at twenty-four people, soon to be twenty-five because I am getting married to my wonderful fiancée this year. And she is one of the best things to ever happen to me. But going back to how I started, it was never really a plan. I never had a business plan, I didn't study fashion, I didn't know anything. I didn't even know how to work a washing machine.

But who needs that when you have YouTube?

I thought in order to really change my life, in order to have something for myself, I had to help myself. I taught myself how to tie-dye with my sister. We would set up tie-dye buckets in the kitchen and my family would get really pissed off because we would make a sh*t-ton of mess and basically stain everywhere.

At this point, I was sixteen years old and I begged my family if I could go and study photography in college, and this college needed zero qualifications. The only qualification you needed was to turn up . . .

But thankfully because I am really successful and business-driven – LOL, I joke – I had no clue what I was doing. I didn't know if this was going to be a career or a hobby. I just made clothes because I just couldn't afford clothes on the high street.

My parents were the kind of parents who made me work for money. I was never given anything even though they are really successful, and I'm so glad they brought me up that way, because it really influenced my outlook on money.

I remember getting work experience in a gym who needed me to take pictures for them. It was kind of like my first ever photography job after college and in return they didn't pay me. It was more like an experience. I thought I was gonna be like a really successful photographer when all I really did was take pictures of flowers outside. But yeah I saw this machine, it's called a vinyl machine and it basically prints off anything. I asked the guy who runs the gym. His name is Wayne Kirk and he was like my business mentor for a few years. He basically said if you do this, I will give you a print.

You can have whatever you want on a T-shirt and at the time there was a really popular brand that I wanted a t-shirt from but could not afford, so we made our own. From this, I looked into making a logo, and then my own prints and then came my own designs. This is where the name Ratchet Clothing came from.

I would then wear it to college and post it on social media. Still at this point I wasn't sure if this was gonna be my forever career as I never sold anything for the first six months, but I remember one night I was going to the cinema and I created this tie-dye sweatshirt. It was half pink and half blue. I took a picture of it on my bedsheet because that was my backdrop. I had posted it on the website, went to the cinema and I didn't really expect any orders. I just didn't really care at this point. I came back and my dad was like you've sold some of these, people on Facebook have commented saying that they've just ordered one and I was like nah can't be, but I checked my PayPal account and in there was £1,000 and I remember the day I saw £1,000 in my PayPal and I literally thought I just won the EuroMillions.

I was like sh*t. Random people I don't know have ordered a sweatshirt that I low-key forgot how I made it. From then, my orders went from two or three a day to around four or five hundred a day. Before I knew it I had my own warehouse, loads of staff, and a young naive me who wasn't money-driven at all, he was just there for the experience. Until 2017 I lost a sh*t-ton of money because I was bored, lost interest in my brand and somehow lost my focus.

I moved to London when I was seventeen to open a store in Lakeside, Essex, where I met one of my best friends, Hussain. He walked into the store, asked me why it was called Ratchet and from there our journey began. He kept telling me to do this and that and even though I hated that sh*t personally, professionally I thought it'd do well for my brand.

It did! I went on tours around the UK, went to fashion shows pretending I gave a sh*t. I even met celebs and gifted clothes to them, people who wouldn't even bat an eyelid at me on the street. It was crazy!!

The older I got, the more I became business-minded and money-driven to make sure my brand was successful. I went through periods of failure and periods of high success. It was all about finding the in-between and making sure I didn't f**k all this hard work up! I had to keep telling myself, help yourself Dhillan!

Some of the highlights in my career were surreal moments, like trending worldwide on Twitter and then meeting Miley Cyrus the week after. Having dinner with David Cameron when he was PM.

My brand is a brand for people who don't really feel like they belong. It's a brand that's built its own community. It's the best community ever. We're all basically a bunch of outcast rejects who have found one another and now we're all a f****d-up happy family. And I wouldn't want it any other way.

If I didn't have such a supportive family I don't think I'd be where I am today. Even though they kinda thought this idea of mine was trash because I was an uneducated child with no hopes (I was lazy and always bored), they did push me to become the best version of myself. And I do love them for it!

But that was a small percentage of why I became so successful. The main reason was because I broke all the rules. I did whatever I wanted to do. I hated listening to other people's opinions. I hate what people have to say.

So my only advice would be to go out there and create your own rulebook.

Everyone's journey is different. Be your own person and do what makes you happy. Everything else will follow, and always remember to HELP YOURSELF.

The Square

FADY ELSAYED

Artist, friend, actor

Hi everyone, my name's Fady Elsayed, I grew up in Islington, North London. I've always aspired to be an actor but I'm not really sure where it came from. I remember growing up a lot of people would say to me I should go to drama school, so I did listen and eventually ended up at one. From there I started doing drama plays and eventually landed with an acting agency.

The role I am going to talk about, instantly I thought it was made for me, but it didn't actually come from my agent but from someone who was a script consultant. They were working with the director of the film, who knew me, and knew they were looking for a young Egyptian actor.

I was seventeen at the time, I'm twenty-nine now. I eventually found out about the audition and went for it, told my agents and everyone was for it. Straight after the audition we went for a family holiday in Egypt. This was my first ever job I had gone up for and a week into my family holiday I got a phone call saying they really liked me and I had to come back for a recall. At the time, I was young, I had never travelled by myself, never got a flight by myself, now I'm speaking to my mum and I'm trying to explain to her this is my dream and I have to go back, her sort of trusting that dream and worried I had to go back myself. Eventually she agreed to let me go back and we were on our way back from a summer chalet driving through the desert and I noticed I didn't have my passport on me. I asked my mum and my family and nobody seemed to have it.

We stopped the car in the middle of the desert and everyone is looking for my passport and nobody can seem to find it. It's really chaotic, my mum is constantly looking in her bag, she can't find it, none of us can. We've rung back to the chalet to see if it's there – it's not. Now we have no passport and I am on a time limit constraint to get back to London from Egypt for my dream job. We then found out you can get an emergency passport from the UK Embassy.

The next day we went to the UK embassy and the first stage was to get documents ready. However, during this period of time the Egyptian revolution was happening and in Tahrir Square where the embassy is, there is a revolution going on, there are millions of protestors on the streets demonstrating and it's really difficult, next to impossible, to get in and around Tahrir Square. We eventually made it through and once in the building we were told we needed to print off a copy of a certain document and the closest place to get this done was outside of Tahrir Square. It was pure chaos at the time so getting out was extremely difficult.

Once we made it out, got the documents ready we were set. However, nobody and I mean nobody was willing to drive us back into where the embassy was located; no taxi was willing to drive us into Tahrir Square, mainly because if you get in, it's virtually impossible to get out.

My mum, bless her, found a taxi driver and prayed for him. I can't really explain it, it would be hard to really do it justice, but she told him she would pray for him and really put her heart on the line for me. It would have been really hard for the taxi driver to say no to her. And he said he was willing to do it for her and wouldn't have considered it for anyone else. He knew going back into Tahrir Square was going to ruin the rest of his day.

We made it back; we were in the building, this was it, the final step. But something was off. There were people mopping and cleaning up the building, it was clearly shut down, everyone had gone home. There was nobody there. I felt gutted, we had done so much to get to this stage and we just missed everyone.

I don't remember the gentleman's name who we saw earlier, but we went up to the second floor where we originally met him. We asked for him but were told he had gone home. My mum was then asked if she was the mother of the boy who needed an emergency passport to go back to London and she said yes, and she was told that the gentlemen we saw earlier left all the paperwork in a file on his desk for us to fill out, sign off and complete to hand in to his colleague.

He gave it to us in a file, we all stood there and were shocked. He really didn't need to do that. He had been working all day in such high intensity, and must have seen hundreds of people that day asking for the same or similar things. He could have easily forgotten about us. But bless my mum and him. My mum must have made an impression on him, because shortly after I got the emergency passport I took all of this energy, flew home alone for the first time in my life. Landed at Heathrow and went straight to recall and got the role!

I got cast for a lead role, which started off my career. I was nominated for a few awards off the back of this performance and it really made me feel like I belonged. Playing a lead role in

My Brother The Devil really changed my life and put my name on the map.

So many people helped me from drama school: acting agents, to the taxi driver, the man in the embassy and of course my dear mum.

A Mother's Guilt

NATASHA ALI

Mother, daughter, sister, assistant headteacher

When they are asleep . . .
When they fall asleep, like really fall asleep; mouth open, eyes
tight kind of sleep you
realise how much of you you'd give to make them happy.
When they are asleep, like really fast asleep, baby dribble down
your top, heavy
breathing type of sleep, you realise how scared you are that you
might not be able to
reach the moon for them.
When they are asleep, like really fast asleep, drifting into a land
far away, you realise
how each night that passes moves at lightning speed and you
can't stop the pace they
are growing up,
Welcome to the world of worry and guilt.
The one you loved and lost goes through your mind.
You want to collect their dreams for them,
Put the rainbow in a jar for them,
Correct all their future mistakes,
Move the stones that may hurt their feet,
Re-define the words that cause them hurt
Fight the sun that might burn
Sit at every table just in case it turns.
Give them your last penny to throw down the well to make

their whimsical but oh so
important wish.
When they are asleep. Like really asleep, lying on your chest
you don't want to breathe
kind of sleep, you realise that you'd die for them if they asked.
But
When they are awake, like really awake, running to the top of
the hill in the playground
and cartwheeling down, you realise you need to step back and
you need to believe in
them . . .
They will fall, the sun will burn,
stones will cut and the rain will pour
but they'll dance in that thunderstorm,
just like you they'll learn to never settle or conform
Wearing the love you've given them as armour
From the moment they were born
They'll transform
And you'll pluck up the courage, you may just join them...
without clutching that umbrella
Go on, what are you waiting for?
Dance with them,
Turn the puddle into an ocean of opportunities
Her love shining down on them
Hope that they become a better version of you
Let them perform their solo . . .

What's The Colour Palette Of Your City?

KIERON BOOTHE

Rapper, artist, friend

Grey clouds over blue skies
Yellow sun for our skin
Yellow lines for our mind
Get with it
Don't park here or you might just get a ticket
Red bus, red blood
Red route, red rum
I think our spirit needs more green spaces.

Sometimes following the GPS isn't the best way to navigate
Be like water and blue will lead the way
There's no solid states when gas turns to ice
Men turn to mice
When everything becomes a franchise
You're the architect for your life
Choose your colours wisely
Don't let it be your demise.

The Art Of Quitting

KIRSTY LATOYA

Digital artist, poet and friend

There's this thing I've been doing recently which I'm thinking about
    quitting
It's not a hobby like drawing, shopping or knitting
It's not a bad habit like smoking or drugs
It's not even a social thing like me spending too much time in
    the clubs

There's no AA meetings for this or groups to assist
Some would say that's a good thing and if I'm being honest I
    am trying to resist

But the truth is I want to give up on life . . .
My mum just died and all these tears I've cried can't even bring
    her back
There's no point in living . . .
But taking my own life would be giving my loved ones more stress
Faces a mess in their new black suit or dress
Wiping their tears as they try to process the tragedy

The gravity of my decision weighs on me
Should I join my angel or try to live comfortably
The worst pain imaginable consumes my being
My cries have no sound any more, I don't even feel alive, I'm
    just being

A few months later I'm asked to vacate
My house of nearly twenty years in seven days
The house that I shared with Mum
Now memories live in boxes that I'm taping up feeling numb
Alone in this world, no parents to guide me

The cloak of depression feels warm beside me
As I contemplate my options, a saviour appears
Not in the form of a person but something I've been doing for
    years

I open my iPad and I start to draw
Stroke by stroke capturing pain so raw
Letting out all the negative emotions
In my own secret creative space going through the motions

My heart is a rainbow so I use it to create
Beauty and pain personified with beautiful brown skin to
    relate
My message ingrained in every piece
'You are not alone' understand this please
I say it to myself while I stand in the mirror
The fog eases up and my reflection seems clearer
This is not the face of a quitter
Life is not all sparkles, sunshine and glitter
But that doesn't mean you give up
This is the face of a warrior so chin up

Art saved my life when I wanted to quit
This gift God gave me, helping me to exist
Healing the world a painting at a time
And telling the story in this little rhyme

I turned my pain into passion and I hope you can do the
  same
I can't wait for your testimony so you can share how great you
  became

Mum's The Word (It's Pretty, Painful)

HUSSAIN MANAWER

The moment after we buried you
Was when it hit me
That there's no-one left to guide me
I became angry, the world kept moving
Cars kept driving, clouds kept floating,
People all around me
But no-one beside me
Mother nature didn't participate
The birds never stopped humming
Time never stopped
My demons kept gunning, they for one saw an opportunity
and didn't wait
I had no idea who I was without you
Absolutely no idea who I was becoming
Feeling my numb heartbeat drumming
Intoxicated
Convincing myself that that was the absolute remedy for grief
and that was the only way
to feel a bit of loving
From myself I was running,
I found it so hard to be discussing
Something linked to you so painfully stunning
That had my blood boiling and rushing
Because a life without you

Had me convinced my life was nothing
I started my healing
When I started accepting
Everything I was revealing
Was everything I was projecting
An underwhelming, overwhelmingly powerful feeling
Had me acting out of character with grief directing
The layers im peeling
Through the scenes I'm selecting
Struggling to find the meaning of the teaching
With all of you I'm detecting but finding it so hard to be
connecting
I'm breathing trying to find the meaning through all I am
dealing
But taught myself I must start respecting
The memories of you I am keeping, whilst pain tries it's best to
be increasing
I'll be ok,
I'll be fine
Because I know you and you loved me
So I'm out here with your love around me protecting
I've turnt to a page in a chapter where you are no longer here
I must move on
But at times forget the sound of your voice
Can't recall the memories as I once could so clear
I try to replay old footage back, but it hurts too much
And for my little heart that's not fair
You may not find me there
But I feel you are still somewhere near
On mum I'm moving and it's no longer confusing
I've come to peace with our grief and even tho I lost you
I know longer feel like I am losing

Lessons They Didn't Teach Me At School

GOODY FROM LEEDS

Poet

The lessons they didn't teach me at school
Were that you shouldn't be surprised
If life is cruel
It won't always be a bed of roses
There will be thorns too
Not everyone will be happy for you
Some will rejoice when you fall
When you hit a wall
Some of the people you thought had your back
Will stab you in it
Others will test you to the limit
Heaven and hell will exist in your mind
Combined
Life isn't easy
Most of it is a grind
To survive
At times you may feel
You don't want to be alive
You will lose people you love
Suffer the pain of unbearable loss
There are many bridges you will have
To cross
But if you can build on the capacity

For resilience
Which resides inside you
You will survive and thrive
And be glad to be alive

The Cube

STEEL BANGLEZ

Record producer

I'll tell you when I wanted to quit.
I built this studio that you're sitting in right now.
Every time, no matter where I travel, I come back to this room.
This room is very sentimental to me.
You know we'd invested a lot of money, etc. etc. I put my all in,
like my body has gone through the trenches like . . . everyone
would come and I couldn't make music bruv. And I thought
you know what, fuck it off. That's the truth bruv. I was sitting
here. There was no Mist, no MoStack, there was none of this
shit, there was nothing. This room was totally different. And it
was the lowest point in my life. But I never let no one know. I
kept it all to me. I just said yeah don't worry there's more.
Don't worry bruv, something's gonna happen like. I just know.

But I haven't gone for therapy, I haven't gone for help, I'm not
on medication, I'm just fighting it in my head and the only way
I made myself happy was listening to old school garage,
watching old school cartoons that I used to watch as a kid, I
tried to bring . . . I tried to do everything . . . that didn't involve
responsibility. You know like before you were awake, before
that.

Man was just chilling here and trying to find some form of
healing through the past and that is actually the story bruv.

And then from there I started making beats and then I met MoStack and the rest is history. But it took me two years to get out of it and I was in this room for two years.

Zinzi And Milo

LUCREZIA MILLARINI

Journalist and friend

There is a meme that keeps appearing on my Instagram feed. Something like 'my dog is not just my friend, he's my best friend'. A cliche, yes, but those clever algorithms have me sussed. In many ways my dog, Milo, really is my best friend.

But what the algorithms won't know is that my connection with animals goes all the way back to my childhood.

I actually grew up with cats. My first was called Zinzi and I loved her more than anything in the world. She was a beautiful long-haired moggie from the local pet shop; our bond was immediate. A surprise gift from my parents, after years of pestering, Zinzi (named after Nelson Mandela's daughter, no less) would follow me around the house, greet me from school every day and curl up to sleep on my pillow every night.

I was eleven and (believe it or not) I was an introvert. Not just the product of being an only child. A classic 'high achiever': on the surface excelling academically, while internally battling with nagging self-doubt and the fear of not achieving my own imposed high expectations. From childhood into teenage years, internalising my emotions became normal to me, but it certainly wasn't healthy.

Zinzi's arrival gave me new purpose and responsibility. I would feed, brush and play with her. In return she would sit with me for hours as I studied for exams, listen attentively while I practised the piano and, above all, her presence was sometimes the only thing that would take away an underlying feeling of sadness that I couldn't really explain, replacing it instead with warmth, patience and unconditional love.

But the 'sadness' I felt as a teenager followed me to university.

I moved from London to Bristol to study law. I had to leave my home, my parents, my beloved Zinzi and, importantly, my routine.

The pressure of needing to achieve and to be the very best at everything returned with a vengeance, taking a brutal and torturous grip on my mind. Again, internalising and feeling overwhelmed, I needed control in my life. I went on to develop an eating disorder and the next three years of my life would be hell. My parents were desperate to remove me from what had become a toxic and dangerous environment, but I was determined to finish what I'd started, despite being so ill. All that time studying, revising and being diligent at school would not go to waste.

And so, I developed a kind of 'plan': study and attend classes in the week, then home for the weekends. Friday afternoons were filled with hope. I would get on that National Express coach knowing that one of the first things I would do when I walked in the door was scoop Zinzi up into my arms and cuddle the life out of her. Even all these years later, I still remember that feeling. Her soft fur on my face, sometimes soaking up tears, but always just happy to see me, whatever my mental state.

God, I loved that cat.

It's the same love I have now for Milo. My gorgeous blond Lhasa Apso, with eyes resembling chocolate buttons. He was a three-month-old puppy, his nose too big for his face, when he joined our compact family unit almost nine years ago. In the time since, he has acquired a certain set of skills including guardian of the cheese drawer, fox poo finder general and, of course, master of the missing sock.

My place in the pecking order is clear: here to provide food, treats, cuddles; and, despite the not-so-welcome occasional bath, I hope to be considered amongst his 'most favourite humans'. But what he will never truly know, in all his infinite wisdom, is just how much I have come to rely on him over the years.

I look back on those tough times at university and I feel an enormous sense of relief that I'm no longer that same person. But I would be lying if I said the 'sadness' had gone away for good. I don't think something like that ever completely leaves a person. I know it has the ability to bubble up every now and then, like a once-dormant volcano, ready to spew its angry lava and throw me off course again.

But as Zinzi was for me then, Milo is for me now as an adult: my emotional anchor. There is nothing I find more soothing or calming than just sitting in the garden next to him as he looks out, listening to every bird that tweets, watching for every squirrel (or indeed brave cat) who happens to wander onto his territory. There is something about his simple enjoyment of nature that makes me stop and also just live in the moment. No matter how stressed or overwhelmed I feel, he is there by my side, anxiously looking up if he senses I'm upset. That look alone is usually enough to bring me back to a better place. What power, what a gift he has!

He is my own personal 'therapy' dog. He won't judge. He doesn't care what I'm wearing, how my career is going or what my 'five-year-plan' is.

There are days when I could easily walk away from my job, but I'd never walk away from him. It is, again, that unconditional love. And we both know it's a two-way thing.

And Yeah, Gratitude

BASHIR 'DOUBLE S' BAZANYE

Music artist

There's so many times that I wanted to quit
Waiting on heaven's door, knowing that the angels exist
The dark times were just moments, so I took me the risks
On a lighter note, I knew it was gonna be lit
There's always light at the end of the tunnel
But in the the circus you juggle
I had to hustle, back to the wall the Jay-Z struggle
You won't understand me if you ain't seen struggle
I've seen it twice so my name's 'Double'
I've seen the bad and the good, I've seen different perspectives
It's how you see it, it's just different selections
You gotta make a decision
On this road, I'm a man on a mission
I won't get lost if I stick to the vision, I see it bird's eyes
You'll never get it right on the first try
Persistence and disciple can make a bird fly
You might turn into an eagle on the third try
This poem is more than a metaphor, it will make your soul fly
I believe in a higher presence
So what I want for my birthday ain't just presents
I show gratitude and get blessings
I ain't a doctor but know how it works, it's just patience
Because these trials and tribulations really tested my faith
Life's a restaurant, my job at the time was to wait

If I work smart the chef will probably chef me a plate
I'm gonna make it I believe in my Fate, that's why I keep me
   the faith

Wickets

HUSSAIN MANAWER

It started after school
With a Bat and a ball all night the boys would be playing
cricket
Under the lamp posts, on side roads, with cars turning in every
minute
Everyone stood around to exhibit
coz Omar had a swing that was so prolific
No1 had a chance against the way Aaron would spin it
Majid, Kieron, all pushed each other to the limit
Through all life took from them
They were determined to take the wickets

The local club just made an announcement
For the boys to join the league
Omar had a placement as an accountant, he couldn't really just
go and join the team
Coach kept saying it in the thousands, you can make it, this is
not a dream
But his Dad weren't around, there's no money to be found, and
this affecting his self esteem

Aaron's sister is battling addiction
More time away is further confliction
There mum has passed and his Dad works hard

Cricket for him is the perfect prescription
He needs to make a decision
To his gut he decides to listen
He sticks to his whites
And decides to follow his vision

Majid's shots are unorthodox
And English is not his first language
Life for him is a paradox
He still plays wearing his bandage
His post trauma, replays in order,
From the days he was left stranded
He signs up to the league with the boys
He's just glad he's got brothers to stand with

Kieron's life has complications,
But you wouldn't really get it from the observations
On medications, following operations
Frustrations for his aspirations
He's never been good at conversations
So he speaks to the the coach of the organisation
That's where he learnt his career had limitations

The league begins
They start to win
Matches home and away
Even though there's boundaries breached
They can't believe
Things are going there way

The league there climbing
It's all aligning

They all wanna watch them play
But there not confiding
Whilst there finding
Their problems at home are to stay

There approaching the semi finals
The outcome could be massive
Aaron can't focus, he's feeling hopeless,
His sister's energy's passive
Just before the big game,
It all kicks off it's dramatic
He finds she's been self harming,
His reaction is all too erratic
And Omar can't figure out
Why his mum is acting so strange
If it's about money, coach has reassured them the sponsor will
pay
She looked him deep in the eye with no words to say
When he left the car door, she whispered to herself may you be
protected today

The cricket club, had an atmosphere, scouts and sponsors,
standing near
Aaron, was late, and Majid can't take all the judgment oh so
near,
Omar went to bowl, and couldn't find the tone, but eventually
got his rhythm there
Coach has noticed, problems floating, but none of the boys
wanna shoot up a flare

Locker room and there changing
Nobody wants to be speaking

Coach is really complaining
Knowing there's feelings, there feeling
The match postponed
Luckily for them it started raining
Coach said *'someone please say something, before you all start leaving'*

Outside we here screaming
As if there's an invasion
They've all run outside to see the what happened
A van pulled up, it's immigration

Majid is in a panic,
Feelings are feeling rapid
Coach stands before him
And says don't worry we'll manage

But what happened next sent shock waves
Through this London Borough
They were there for Omar
It's hell all over this summer
He tried to run, but got out done,
As he hears the screams of his mother
He gives himself in, unable to think,
What life would now discover

It started after school, with a Bat and a ball all night the boys
would be playing cricket,
under the lamp posts, on side roads, with a car turning in every
minute
Everyone stood around to exhibit, coz Omar had a swing that
was so prolific,

No1 had a chance against the way Aaron would spin it,
Majid, Kieron, all pushed each other to the limit
Through all life took from them, they were determined to take
the wickets

Save Obaid

OBAIDULLAH AND QAMAR JABARKHYL

Student

It is the summer of 2021 and nine-year-old Obaid and his family have to flee their home in the Nangarhar province of Afghanistan. Up to that point they had been living a peaceful life, but then Obaid's father and cousins received death threats directly from the Taliban for working with the Republican Government supporting the NATO mission that was designed to help maintain stability and security in Afghanistan.

Obaid's extended family members in the UK were working with the British authorities to help facilitate an evacuation plan; the family were advised to meet at the Baron Hotel, a secure compound next to the airport in central Kabul, where thousands had fled to escape.

After a few restless days of waiting, an unexpected bomb blast shook Obaid's world. Amidst the chaos, smoke and screams, Obaid, his twin brother Irfanullah and an elderly relative became detached from the rest of their wider family and they were flown to Doha, Qatar, for safety.

Panicked, worried and scared, they arrived at Doha Airport to even more turmoil.

Tired and exhausted, Obaid fell asleep on the airport floor. The next thing he knew, he was shaken awake by a stranger and directed onto a plane with no idea where he was going. Obaid frantically searched for his twin, but Irfanullah was nowhere to be seen.

Alone on a plane and unable to speak the language, relying on the words of strangers that he did not understand, Obaid was terrified. The strangers reassured him he would be reunited with his brother once the plane landed. However that night, it landed in France. Obaid was still desperately searching the crowds for his twin when he was ushered onto a bus to another unknown destination: Strasbourg.

There, word spread of the little Afghan boy with no family and reached a 22-year-old Afghan refugee, who saw similarities between himself and Obaid. He took Obaid in and agreed to be his guardian. While under guardianship, it was Obaid's tenth birthday. A cake was bought for him, but he was unable to cut it. He sobbed and yearned to be reunited with his family.

Unbeknownst to Obaid, his family were still stranded in Kabul, unable to leave the airport; but his twin, Irfanullah, had miraculously been evacuated correctly and reunited with loved ones in London.

In the UK, Irfanullah and his relatives were constantly trying to raise awareness with local MPs in an attempt to contact the Home Office, while trying their best to get Obaid's story to the mainstream media to gain wider attention.

The guardian who was helping Obaid realised that being his full-time guardian while having to work long hours was no longer possible. Alone once again, Obaid, now aged ten, was handed over to a refugee camp that was to become his home for the longest five weeks of his young life.

Living in the camp was not easy. Obaid recalls the place not being nice at all, especially for a child. There were limited resources, no play areas, no games, no good food, and no proper bedding. Each room housed four people with two people sharing each bed and with the oldest person in the room aged thirty.

Despite the horrid conditions, Obaid never ever gave up hope and neither did his family. Obaid's cousin in the UK, Qamar Jabarkhyl, had been in communication with MP Bob Blackman for Harrow East. Mr Blackman began making enquiries to the Home Office and confusion began growing as for some reason the case had been closed in December 2021. Blackman then went on to raise the case in the House of Commons, which helped to gain media interest. With the first press interview going viral, awareness grew and action began.

On the grey morning of 7 September 2022, the Eurostar train from France arrived at King's Cross St Pancras. Obaid stepped onto British soil and into the waiting arms of his brother Irfanullah; his cousins and uncles were there carrying flowers, toys, clothes and gifts.

Obaid is currently doing well at school in the UK. He has dreams and goals to attend university and study for a degree in either medicine or engineering.

Obaid's father has been missing since December 2021. The Taliban deny any involvement. Obaid's mother and the rest of his family are still trying to flee Afghanistan. In July 2023 a family reunion application was submitted for approval to the Home Office. Save Our Citizenships, a grassroots organisation, learnt about the plight of Obaid and his family. They helped raise media awareness and supported the fundraising efforts enabling visits for family members from the UK to check in with Obaid while he was in France. The Save Our Citizenships team were also present as Obaid stepped off the train, glad to welcome him and help him feel at home here in the UK.

An Account Of Pakistan Floods

HUSSAIN MANAWER

Throughout the winter months of September–December 2022, myself and my dear high school friend Luqman Khan embarked on three trips to Pakistan to do what we could to help those impacted by the floods. Another lifelong friend, Amir Awan, joined the first trip, with film-maker Jack Harries joining the third. With the power of social media we managed to fundraise £60,000 to help.

Thank you boys, for everything you all did on these missions to deliver aid, for your time, love and generosity.

Thank you also to everyone who donated throughout the fundraising period.

Another special thank you is to Saifullah Afridi for driving them long distances in the heat, for taking care and looking after us every moment of the day and night, much love my brother.

Brother Naeem Afridi , thank you also, for your care and consideration on our trips. Your guidance was extremely valuable and your love held no bounds.

And to Brother Adnan Raz at Alkhidmat Foundation, you do such incredible work, you show the spirit of Pakistan and charity in its purest light, thank you.

This passage of the book is an account of our journey to try to help, stories first hand from those on the ground who survived one of the world's deadliest floods due to climate change in 2022 and what needs to be done, now, to help.

FROM BELGRAVE ROAD TO
TERMINAL 3 HEATHROW

It's the evening of Thursday 8 September 2022 and I'm sitting with two of my close friends, Ikram and Amir, at Amir's family home and we stumbled across a video on YouTube that showed that Pakistan had been hit with a disastrous flood, impacting the lives of multiple millions of people. We sat heartbroken, confused, concerned and wanting to do something. I suggest setting up a GoFundMe page and Ikram said, 'Bruv you will raise a lot of money, make sure you set a high target,' followed by Amir saying, 'Yeah, and let's go ourselves to help.' Almost instantly, I called another dear friend of mine, Luqman, and said, 'We need to go Pakistan, we need to do something to help.' He immediately dropped everything and days later we found ourselves boarding a flight at Heathrow Airport to Islamabad.

Eight hours later, upon landing, we meet Saifullah (a member of Luqman's family), who has also come to help.

We left Islamabad to drive a two-and-a-half-hour car journey to Peshawar, which is in the province of Khyber Pakhtunkhwa, where we were scheduled to meet Adnan and the team at the Alkhidmat Foundation. We began viewing a map of the flood-affected areas and noticed some areas were hours away from roads, limiting access to them. I then questioned and said, 'What happens here? What happens to the people that live here?'

We were informed that many areas were not only hard to get to due to there not being roads, but the journey to these areas posed a serious risk of threat, due to robbery, heavy fog and mist, lack of light after sunset, theft of aid and also potential hazards due to lack of road structure.

We discussed it and decided these hard-to-reach places are

where we are meant to go. Maybe the inner saviour complex in us developed an ego, but it didn't matter, we were determined to get to people who really needed help. After sitting in a meeting room at the foundation's office for hours, we made a plan: that the aid was to travel the night before us, so we wouldn't have anything on us in case of a robbery, we would hire off-road vehicles to help cope with and handle the lack of road structure, and we planned to leave early in the morning to travel as many hours of the night to maximise our time in daylight.

We were set to travel to the Dera Ismail Khan district, where the relentless downpour of heavy monsoon rain and merciless floods have ravaged villages, destroying infrastructure and amongst this, taking precious human life.

With international calls to our friends, family members and colleagues back home we, collectively with the team at the Alkhidmat Foundation, developed a comprehensive plan for the funds raised. Our strategy consisted of a two-tier operating system:

Part One: Providing Immediate Aid
- 1,500 mosquito nets (holding two people)
- 700 food packages (consisting of daal, kidney beans, salt, sugar, rice, flour, tea, jelly, mango juice, water and oil) reaching approx 4,900 people
- 20 medical pop-up day camps with qualified doctors providing medicine and hygiene kits, seeing approx 350–400 people a day
- 10,000 hot cooked meals of potato and rice

Part Two: Developing A Long-Term Sustainable Plan
- The development of four solar-panelled sustainable wells to

be dug at 1,000 feet deep, providing fresh drinking water for up to 4,000 people, cattle, farming and crops. The wells to be protected with walls and gates in case of future flooding.

We got a night's sleep and headed out in the morning at around 5 a.m. A six-to-seven-hour drive down one of South Asia's longest and oldest roads, the Grand Trunk Road. Also known as the GT Road, it is an ancient pathway that stretches approximately 1,600 miles, and in itself it is an extremely important symbol of cultural, geographical and historical significance. It reaches various cities throughout Afghanistan, Pakistan, India and Bangladesh, including Kabul, Peshawar, Rawalpindi, Islamabad, Lahore, Amritsar, Delhi, Kolkata, West Bengal, Dhaka, Gazipur, Tangail to name a few.

Within moments it became impossible to not notice that 'lack of road structure' was not a light statement, as sixteen-wheeler trucks lay helplessly overturned, the road embedded with uneven large-scale unpredictable potholes, cliff-edge drops, people sleeping in the middle beneath any shade they could find, random police stops, signs of rock slides. I had no idea what to make of this. But through travelling down this ancient highway, I thought, *Where are all the aid trucks? Why can't I see anyone else in charity vests?* It started to become painfully evident that there was an extreme lack of support attempting to reach those who really need it.

Once off the GT Road, we entered DI Khan and continued for a further three hours off road. A bumpy, hard-hitting commute took us deeper into the heart of many villages within this province. As we travelled further, paved roads turned to stone roads, to sand roads, to eventually no road. Our vehicle was scratched by numerous thorn-ridden branches from all directions the closer we were getting to our destination, with our driver turning and saying to us 'No car has been down here in a very long time.'

Once the bushes and branches eased up, we began passing the bones of many deceased animals: skulls, ribcages of buffalo, goats, cattle, as they lay out on the road beside us; and then, the monster itself. The flood water, stagnant, dominant, stubborn with its sinister presence, ignoring nature's and science's laws of evaporation despite being under this intense heat, holding firm onto its newfound territories.

A meeting of water none of us will ever forget.

As I asked how much of a drive we have left, we suddenly stopped, and the car filled with an instant silence as heartbreak revealed itself. A young father with his two young children kneeling down to drink from this infected, dirty, contaminated water while filling up buckets of this murky liquid to travel back home with.

My heart began pounding and I wanted to scream, 'Don't drink that, what are you doing?' But who am I to say anything, as I clutch a half-empty mineral water bottle in my lap, with a neck pillow, and an iPhone.

This man is trying to survive, he is trying to provide for his family in these extremely difficult circumstances. I couldn't believe it. And to further upset the children had no trousers, they had no undergarments, they were unshielded, they couldn't be older than three or four, unequipped, unprepared and half naked. Toddlers, who have had their rightful childhood robbed. These children have been forcefully propelled to the unforgiving frontline of this climate calamity; they should be living carefree with joyous moments of blissful youth and innocence, but instead they carry a weight of fear and danger far beyond their years, invisible but evident through their powerful stunning eyes. A sip away from further infection.

As our car slowly began to drive to our destination and the father smiled goodbye to us, my heart felt a heaviness I hadn't ever experienced, indescribable. My mouth was unable to formulate words, my brain pounding against my skull: *How on earth is this allowed to happen? Where is the global outrage? Where is the international community? Where is HELP?!*

The vehicle stopped, surrounded by mud huts, straw, smoke, dust, ash, heavy stones and what looked like a pond. I turned round to see a group of young children dancing within the smoke that our car had caused as if it was a special treat for them. And as the dust settled they stared at me. I couldn't look them in the eyes at first and, when I did, I attempted a smile and they smiled back and ran over to us, to see if we had any gifts for them.

We did, we planned for this, we had sweets . . .

I then felt sick to my stomach, handing out sweets to children in this horrific situation. One, two sweets each. Even though our aid activities were set up, I wanted to help more.

The emotions within me were massively conflicting and clashing. By this point the rest of the village had come around our vehicle to see what was going on and my eyes were fixated on a group of young girls walking with empty buckets on their heads. They were laughing and joking with each other and then slowly began picking up pace, running, chasing each other towards the water; they each removed the bucket from their head and placed it beside them and began filling it up with water. This was not a pond, this was not a well or a reservoir, it was flood-infected water that had set in the middle of this village.

A norm so horrifying that every single home to the local people's knowledge now has waterborne diseases within it. Riddled with infections, bacteria, parasites, viruses and, to add to this, hovering throughout the sky mosquitoes and flies. The lack of access to clean drinking water is now fulfilling a cycle of suffering, despite the fact that these people have already lost absolutely everything.

I walked closer towards the water, I saw dogs swimming within it, I saw frogs, I saw dirt, filth, and so much more. It was at this moment that a local man approached me and said, 'This water you are seeing is the same water we clean the bodies of our dead relatives in when they pass. And so many have been passing lately.' I looked stunned, even more so because the line that followed pierced.

They were upset that when they presented themselves to their God when they died, they would be doing so having not washed in clean water.

I was speechless, that the pain of this life is following them into the next.

After we had distributed some sweets and biscuits, the elders in the village came to walk us over to the part of the land that we had purchased from the money fundraised to begin construction on this solar panel well.

We measured the land with a rope, said a prayer and began digging. They called this a 'groundbreaking process'. I, for one, felt so many emotions of extreme utter privilege versus sadness amidst a sense of self-entitlement.

How much this well would do for this community of people, animals and their crops was truly evident. The majority of them are farmers, and the floods took their crops and by taking the crops took their livelihoods and life as they knew it. As we headed inside a mud hut and sat on a string of straw beds, the elders of the village appointed a spokesman on their behalf.

Very professional, well mannered, he welcomed us and the words that came from his mouth rang hardhitting, raw, hopeful and true.

'Our government has forgotten us, the world has forgotten us, people speak of villagers as uneducated people, they say that we are best to be left, our women are ill, our children are starving, we have heard you travelled far to help, thank you.'

My response was: 'I'm glad you accepted our help and it is by no way in any shape or form enough, we will come back, we will raise more money, this is not it, I'm so sorry.'

Introducing: Mulazim Hussain

My name is Mulazim Hussain. The deadly floods hit this area, which brought destruction on a large scale. Children and animals (in particular) are badly affected. The crops on the other hand have also been acutely destroyed. There are no proper roads that we use for transportation. The water level is almost seven feet, which caused massive destruction. There are approximately five hundred homes in this area and all have been affected by the devastating floods. The entire infrastructure is badly damaged such as schools, madrassa etc. We humbly request the government and NGOs to assist us at this critical juncture so that the things may get normal. Clean drinking water is one of the worst problems here as there is scarcity of drinking water. I, on behalf of the entire community, appeal to government and NGOs to please come forward to render clean drinking water and that shall be possible only when we have water of our own. There is no hospital in the vicinity, so we take the patients to a distant hospital, which itself is a Herculean task as there is no passage that can be called a road. Women and children sometimes die right in the middle of the way being carried to the hospital.

Introducing: Inam Ullah

My name is Inam Ullah and I belong to this area, which has been completely damaged by the flood of August 2022. It was evening when the fatal flood hit us. We hardly survived ourselves and the cattle as there is no proper transportation and roads. The time we came back after we survived, all our houses had totally perished. It was impossible for us to even walk because there was seven to eight feet flood water. The government primary school was completely damaged and the kids are now getting education under the shadow of the trees. Apart from this there is no dispensary and doctor here. Due to the unavailability of the hospital, our patients (pregnant women in particular) sometimes die on the way because of no roads. We hardly carry our patients to DI Khan. The condition of the sewerage system and the streets is alarming. Shelter is one of our basic needs. We humbly demand from the government agencies and the NGOs to help us in this critical time. Shelter, dispensary and school need to be established on a priority basis. This is what we demand from the government and NGOs.

Introducing: Ranjha

My name is Ranjha and I have six children. The flood of 2022 was a horrible day of my life. The deadly flood that hit the area washed ashore each and everything. Our houses, school, madrassa and the rest of the infrastructure has totally been damaged. I am working on daily wages nowadays while before I owned my own shop, which has been destroyed by the disastrous flood that hit the area. When the flood came, we had nothing to

*eat and drink. Our herd of cattle perished in a flash of time
which was my source of income. The weather here is quite hot
just like a blazing inferno. In short, life has totally changed after
the flood. In short the flood severely impacted our lives that
can't be properly mentioned in words. I request the government
and NGOs to help us in this time of trial.*

Listening to their stories, standing amongst their broken
homes, the demolition of their villages and lives, it was
abundantly clear that their strength, willpower, faith, love and
human spirit is truly remarkable. Once they finished speaking
they provided us with gifts of beautiful fabric, they wrapped it
on our heads and crowned us spokesmen for them and then as
they heard we were coming they left the little meat they had
and cooked it for us.

We then told them we couldn't eat their food. The village
elders took offence. The same thing happened with the cloth. I
told them, we can't take this, but then decided to make a
promise instead.

I said hold on to this piece of fabric for when I come back,
and when I come back I will take it then. Because I will come
back, we will come back. I have never felt more love anywhere
else on this planet than I have stood amongst these people,
their eyes holding depths consisting of compassion, love and
fight. I then turned to one man and said, 'I feel guilty because
even still in this situation I am getting something from it.'

I then asked if they would pray with us? They agreed, we
prayed, we said our goodbyes, and as we did it became very
emotional.

Just before we left, Luqman and Amir noticed a young child
with a very serious ear infection, but he had no money for
treatment. As we offered to take care of it, he told us about

another child whose infection was worse than his and that child needed it more. We ensured his ear treatment was taken care of and left funds for the other child also.

There is so much more to be done here. This not only is one of the greatest disaster tragedies of all time, the aftermath and what has followed it and the lack of aid is a huge violation of international human rights. It must be addressed: immediate aid, sustainable solutions, help is needed. Not just in Pakistan; all across the world there are people suffering through causes that they individually or collectively as a community played no role in causing.

This all stemmed from a promise my mother made me make many years ago. She made me promise her, if I was ever in a position given a platform and voice, *I must do what I can to help feed the world.*

And that leads me to end this chapter of help with a poem I wrote on my way to the airport getting dropped off by Luqman and his dear mother, called 'Phir Milenge', which translates to 'We Will Meet Again'.

Phir Milenge (We Will Meet Again)

When the glaciers melt
When the water drums
When the rain doesn't help
When the world doesn't love

Phir Milenge

When the animals fall
When the trees tumble
When homes are rocked
When baby feet touch rumble

Phir Milenge

When hope ring the way it could
When help does come through the way it should
When those who can never would

Phir Milenge

When dust fills the sky
When the soil in the earth runs dry
When the clouds burst and can't control their cries
When humanity needs a gravestone because it has died

Phir Milenge

When medicine is a mother's kiss
When childhood is a gift that's been stripped
When fatherhood is ripped
When your circumstance makes you externally poor but
internally rich
Phir Milenge

We will meet again

Phir Milenge

PART FIVE

Healing

DOCTOR POETRY

HUSSAIN MANAWER

NIHAL ARTHANAYAKE

LIONESS

THE UNWED WIFE

HARRIS J

MIST

MARIAH IDRISSI

M.MUSE

PARIS CHONG

MORRISSON

KSI

OLLY WILLIAMS

SAM TOMPKINS

FREDDIE PEARSON

EBONEE DAVIS

JOHN BURTON

MAX BOWDEN

SARAH CALLAGHAN

MEGGAN ROXANNE

SAIDA AHMED

ANDREA THOMPSON

A Poem From The Rhythmic Ward

DOCTOR POETRY

Head of the rhythmic ward

I pray that happiness does its best to try to

Lead you to a place where faith does guide you

I will forever pray that time is kind too

And all the love you created and left in pockets of our planet
finds you, to bind you,

With peace and tranquillity

Safety and stability
For your gentle and your humility

Your comfort and prosperity
Your generosity and sincerity

For all you've done and all you keep doing for the children of
the world and humanity

Emotionally, your currency holds legacy,
memorably, keep manifesting and creating your chemistry,

I WANTED TO QUIT TOO

Protect your weaponry
We're artists, we are dangerously sensitive, preciously

But the melody's the remedy
Allow it to guide you mentally

I Will Be There

HUSSAIN MANAWER

I don't know where to begin
What do I say?
Your strong if you know this chronicle

If you had to leave the home you were raised
Your outbursts are logical

New sounds around
Rest your crown
The first night can be horrible
The first week diabolical
You've earnt you badge and it's honorable

You can't afford to hibernate
None of this is pathetic
I need you to find a way
To cover the gas and electric
We've got left overs in the microwave
Your hurt i'm not saying forget it
I'm home sick too
And here's a home truth
If you don't move you will never get it

I'll be there in the nighttime, words are a lifeline, for when

grief comes knocking
When ur not in the right mind, and u hit a landmine, for all the
tears ur dropping
On the outline, ur offline, and depression rocking
But there ain't no sunshine, for a real long time, ur blessings i
cant have u blocking

Listen to me, you got this and i'm not just being polite
the bags are under ur eyes, are souvenirs from the nights you
had no choice to fight
I know your closest don't no this
you battled all your life
You wear pain so well,
That your numb and it don't feel nice

I need you to keep on working, when grief is bursting, now
that your on your journey
Your valid it's hurting and it's disturbing but trust me when i
say your worthy
When there's demons smirking, the judgment's burning, I'll be
your power of attorney
Whilst your spirit is yearning coz your soul needs nursing now
that the road of healing can be blurry

Through generations, we've had limitations, on being strong
and survival
We need conversations, For the complications , if your ever
feeling suicidal
A new formation manifestations let's destroy the cycle
I'll be there for you, but you need to be there too, trust me,
when i'm telling you it's vital

I know healing can feel like it's quite far
But todays the day that it might start
On this cold play, there's an ever glow
Hidden amongst the night stars
Protect yourself, on your right guard
In the deep end, there's no lifeguard
Some of your closest don't realise
That everyday you die hard

I understand that i don't understand
The emotions that are arising
What i do no is what i will do
That's to be with you when it's frightening
When the devil take a liking
To PTSD when it's heightening
I will turn up ready, with love so heavy
I say well done for all the crying

To tell you the truth, i dunno what to do i don't wanna be
overly positive
I'm reading the room, There's time to be happy, but right now
we need the opposite
It doesn't make you toxic in this story, for a moment your not
the optimist
Work your emotions, before they work you, you don't need to
be an apologist

We take big breaths with small steps I know my baby it's painful
No less, that's progres, demons always want angels

Lets flip the script, and fight for this, to yourself you can't be
hateful

Your doing so well, for your mental health, we do gratitude
daily, grateful

Through generations, we've had limitations, on being strong
and survival
We need conversations, For the complications , if your ever
feeling suicidal
A new formation manifestations let's destroy the cycle
Ill be there for you, but you need to be there too, trust me,
when i'm telling you it's vital

Invisible

HUSSAIN MANAWER

You are a song I've never heard of
Words I'm yet to spell
A chapter I can't wait to turn to,
Where it's not me by myself
You can come out whenever
Lord knows, I've been waiting long enough
But you don't need to be invisible my darling
Because, that don't work for us

I'm yearning for you to wake me up
As i'm wrapped up in my sheets
I wanna tell you all about life
And what that thing really did to me
I picture what your name is
I change it through the time
I pray to God you are everything, I'm hoping one day
I'm gonna find

You are a song i've never heard of
Words I'm yet to spell
A chapter I can't wait to turn to,
Where it's not me by myself
You can come out whenever
Lord knows, I've been waiting long enough

But you don't need to be invisible my darling
Because, that don't work for us

I just gave up dreaming
But i've stayed believing
That you will come right over here and fix the way I'm feeling
But you see my thoughts, began to tell me
I deserve this lonely
So i turn from anyone
Who would try to hold me
You are a song i've never heard of
Words I'm yet to spell
A chapter I can't wait to turn to,
Where it's not me by myself
You can come out whenever
Lord knows, I've been waiting long enough
But you don't need to be invisible my darling
Because, that don't work for us

A Letter To Myself

NIHAL ARTHANAYAKE

Broadcaster, author and semi-retired DJ

Hi Nihal,

It's Nihal.

You have just started secondary school and you are terrified.
The first morning has gone badly. You decided to go straight
onto the upper deck of the school bus and that was a big
mistake. You are the younger sibling and alongside your
brother the only other Asian on the bus. The kids are
fascinated by you and swarm around you as you take your seat.
Nobody told you that the upper deck was the space reserved
for the rowdier kids, the ones who have dominion over those
who choose the safer environment of the lower floor. These
boys and girls smell the fear emanating from you as sharks
sense the blood of a stricken creature in the water. They pick
you apart, socks, shoes, trousers, jumper, glasses. Nothing
escapes their notice or derision. And there you are, having the
confidence eroded from without. It is a morning that you will
never forget. The realisation dawns that you cannot and will
not be a victim. A map will have to be drawn that will teach
you to navigate the playground like a new MP has to when
entering the House of Commons. The bullies avail themselves
very quickly. They are either to be avoided or befriended.
Humour works: a quick wit can also aid survival but that wit

should never be used to demean or patronise them. Do not underestimate them. Make sure they owe you, and never owe them.

The first boy who calls you the 'P word' is called Desmond. He is regarded to be one of the toughest in the year. Before you are aware of the phrase 'the best form of defence is offence' you employ it. You fight him. Neither of you win but he knows that you are not Mahatma Gandhi, even though he has no idea who Gandhi-ji is. You are a Brown boy in a white world and craving allyship. There are white boys who are willing to back you up, and a Black boy called Leon. He has an older brother so he is protected, and you come into the orbit of that protection.

Nobody at your school is told that they will end up running the world. The village, town and school you inhabit suffocates you. You want to be anonymous in a big city. There is something about this genre of music called hip hop that sees you. This culture, which is still only a decade old, speaks to you about culture, politics, art, dance and language. You are fourteen years old. You are listening to a man rap about a place called the Bronx in New York. There is more affinity with a stranger recording a song in New York full of bravado than there is with 99 per cent of the kids you go to school with. Because the rapper is a person of colour and all the people of colour you know seem always to be on the defensive, cowering, trying to assimilate for protection. Hip hop makes you feel empowered.

Whenever you fail, you accept it. In trying to fit in and be popular you sacrifice academic results. What is cool at school has no merit or power in the real world, but if anybody had told you that then you would have ignored them. Your exam results are not good. A CDE in your A levels means that it is the lottery of clearing and scraping into an academic institution that you had previously never heard of. But you are free of a small town, and a mentality that confines you to a lack of ambition. You believe in connecting people, helping them. There is a word for what you do and for some it is a derogatory one. You are a networker. As I look back across your/my life I know one thing: that every reason to quit was overruled by an optimism that came with connecting with people. You never put out positivity hoping for something in return. It is never immediately transactional. Although it does return to you, trust me.

There is a discovery that you will make later on in life when many people will approach you and talk about how you helped them, believed in them, gave them your time and advice. Even though you have battled with insecurities and impostor syndrome, others will help you realise that homogeneity is the enemy of creativity and your experiences and ideas matter, you are in every room you are in because you deserve to be there. When you get older you will learn that your experiences have currency. Be curious and open and others who share those character traits will be drawn towards you. Quitting is a privilege; you don't have that option. Just keep it moving and you will prevail.

Yours with much love,

Nihal

The Shade I'm In
LIONESS

Artist and friend

Don't worry, I wanted to quit too . . .
. . . and I actually went through with it,
I let someone else's view depict,
What became my next move, was it,
Because they actually had a point?

'Lioness would be better if she was light-skinned.'

So hold on, my ability to create music would be enhanced if I
    had a lighter skin tone?
It's nonsense but the seed had been thrown,
And then poof, doubt had been grown,
Coz now I don't feel so marketable,
Forget talent, that's not even half of the pull,
What's the point, I'm done, had to part from it all,
But guess what? You stand taller after a fall,
So I don't regret a single thing,
I went away,
got thicker skin,
Loved me more in the shade I'm in,
And if they shade me now, they can't break within.

What Is Happiness?
THE UNWED WIFE

LMK – Founder of Pachee

I remember when we met at 14
In our school dinner hall
You told your sister you were in love
I just kept my cool
Fast forward 10 years and we travelled the world
Soon after in my belly, a baby was curled

I never had a father, watching you father
was a blessing to be
Now our son is the one in the same
Position as me
Ironically that would kill you just to know
You've left your baby boy all alone

And what can I say about us
We were joined at the hip
For 16 years you would catch me when I slip
That safety net was taken away
I still don't know how I left you in that hospital bay
I think about that EVERY single day

We learned so much from one another
For me it was facing my fears
For you it was watching musicals
And not having to hold back tears

Now we are left with our memories and triggers
I remember when stress was
planning all 3 of our dinners
Oh how I wish I could just watch you eat
While watching a movie, you playing with my feet

Heartache doesn't get better in time
Your consistently reminded of your previous life
What keeps me going is our son and family
His smile and their strength through their agony

Although being social has taken a while
I'm not convinced this is happiness
it's more like depression with a smile

You Have To Hurt To Heal

HARRIS J

Artist, dear friend

Quitting cannot be an option. If it's an option then you've already lost.

You have to go into things with optimism, confidence and positive thinking. There was a time in my life where I gave up on everything. I've been gifted and blessed with so much, so looking back it doesn't make sense to me how I could overlook all of that. But before you know it you've fallen into a pit and have no idea how to get out.

No matter how many people are around you, you feel completely alone. You have days where you're smiling and happy but there's a constant dark cloud hanging over you waiting to consume you. No one can get through to you. You've trapped yourself in a prison that only you have the key for.

But you do have the key. The key is in lying in all the places that your mind is telling you you don't want to go. For me I know I need to allow my heart to guide me through things, and weather a storm that my brain can take me away from at that time, but ends up leaving me further inside a pit of darkness.

The brain is an amazing thing, but it's rational, and rationality isn't always the best answer. We have to be hurt to heal. You can't heal a wound that won't show itself. Let yourself discover your wounds by allowing yourself to feel whatever it is you're running away from.

It might seem like the worst thing to do at the time but you will be thanking yourself later on. I believe we are defined by how we take ourselves out of these dark times in our life. Life is a test and we only know what we're made of when we're confronted with something that feels like it's too hard but is actually exactly what we need to be able to progress into the next stages of life.

It's exactly how I feel, but I find it so much easier to say it than do it. However, I know I'm only able to know this because I'm going through it.

After Pain Comes Strength
MIST

Rapper

February 2011, I'm nineteen years old and I just had a child.
August, a few months later, and my dad experienced a sudden
heart attack and sadly passed away. Three months passed and
in November, my mum had a sudden brain aneurysm and I lost
her too. I was nineteen, I went from a yard where my mum was
doing everything for me, ironing my clothes, cooking dinners
every day to now being responsible for bills and a mortgage. I
wasn't inclined for that way of life and because I never paid,
following all of this, our family home got repossessed.

Being a lad and being nineteen it's so easy to get caught up
in things. My area was gang-affiliated but I wasn't. I loved
motorbikes and cars, all the mad sh*t. I got into a lot of trouble
for driving, because I was doing so before I was actually
allowed to drive, and that eventually got serious to the point I
was sentenced to fourteen months' prison. I never thought I'd
go to prison, I just thought my ban would be extended. I was
on a two-year ban, got caught driving, got given another
two-year ban, got caught driving, and before you knew it with
no licence. I tried to get away; I got incarcerated.

I was around twenty-three, twenty-four at the time and my
daughter was four years old. I was in prison, with no trade
behind me. I then began the process of rehabilitation. I was in
this class and the first question was 'Who are you?' Who am I?
It was presented to me on a spider diagram. It was asking me

to list things as to who I am, and the woman leading the class said she didn't want things on there like 'I'm a brother, a dad, a friend'. I remember her clearly saying, 'I want you to write, who you are as a person.'

I started looking around the room, giving a geezer next to me the side-eye, trying to see what he was writing. And after looking around the room I realised, nobody is writing anything. One guy eventually got up and said he was a builder, and as they went round one funny guy said he was a human. Everyone laughed at that. There were around six or seven people that didn't write anything. I was one of them. I then kept thinking, 'Sh*t, what can I actually write?'

Eventually she let us write down things such as 'I'm a dad, brother, son', and that's all I was able to write. I went back to my cell and I took the booklet I was working on. Being in the cell you get very bored, you read, you start doing things you wouldn't normally do. I kept looking back at this booklet thinking, 'Why couldn't I write who I am? What the hell is going on?' At that moment a brainwave hit me. I started thinking, 'What am I actually doing with my life? How couldn't I even write who I am? What life is this I am living?' In prison you get certain certificates for taking up subjects. I did English and maths again, as well as information technology and business studies. This helped a lot, especially as I got excluded from school in Year Nine, I got caught smoking and they didn't play with me, no suspension or nothing; they kicked me out straight away. So from Year Nine I didn't go to school. Doing this education in prison really got my brain back in gear, it was really mad for me. This process started making me want more out of life. The best classes that really helped me were maths, getting into sums, and business studies, which helped me develop the vision of wanting to become an entrepreneur. I started generating ideas of setting up a burger van, a shisha bar, a sweet company, dessert shops, they were all ideas I was having. It gave me drive. I had things to look forward to.

When I came out of prison, I needed a fixed address. But because I was living here, there and everywhere I had to move into a hostel. Then my independence started growing and stability followed. I was building, I got my passport sorted, my birth certificate, I got all the identification I needed for life. But it was back in prison I started rapping. I started writing raps and had a few beats and while in the hostel, Cobain said, 'Yo, you're cold man' and he had a mate that works for P110, the broadcasting music platform, and for £150 he got me a onetake music video where I started rapping. It got put up online and from there, it didn't stop . . .

I did a few grime things back in the day when I was younger but a lot of people thought I was either dead or in prison. It was mad, it was like a redemption. I was bringing a sound that they didn't know was missing and now people have got it and they're happy. Good comments and feedback started coming in, so I just decided to crack on. There was a thing at the time, where if your video gets a certain amount of views they give you a free scene smasher. I managed to get 200,000 views and then delivered a scene smasher. From that moment, God rest his soul Jamal Edwards reached out. He just got his MBE from the Queen and I sat there thinking, 'Jamal who got an award from the Queen just hit me up!' It was a big highlight for me. He asked me what I thought about doing a freestyle for SBTV, and after that Charlie Sloth hit me up and offered too, and to turn up on that platform was really crazy. I remember being in prison listening to Fire in the booth, so to come out and accomplish that was crazy.

I then had this idea to do big video, mind-blowing videos; I did one in Dubai then managed to do one in Iceland. And after that the recognition really started coming from the back of music and it was really rewarding knowing that the hard work was being noticed.

Another moment that followed from that point was the 'Diamond in the Dirt' tour. It sold out quite fast and to be honest it's surreal for me. Doing a tour and seeing all of my loyal fans at these shows really reminded me that I came from nothing. To have all these people come to each city, to see thousands of people reciting my lyrics, watching the reactions, made me understand whatever I'm doing is actually amazing and people respect it. It was a wakeup call, it really allowed me to understand them.

When it's been hard I always remind myself that with pain comes strength. If you get through the pain stage and grieving stage it gives you strength and it makes you stronger. Whenever you come out on the other side of anything that's hard or whenever you're going through something it's there to teach you a lesson. Even the hard things and the bad things we have to go through, it's all lessons learnt.

I tend to drive past my old family home all the time. If I'm with people as well to show them, the journey and the atmosphere of where I grew up. There's been so much growth and for me to have my own TV show and be where I am is crazy. I've learnt as well, with regards to the journey of healing. We can sometimes get so busy and caught up with things in life we forget about ourselves. I think the main thing in life is taking care of yourself and then everything else will follow nicely. Without taking care of yourself there's no taking care of anyone else. Even though things such as good food and making time to go to the sauna are important, it's important to take care of yourself.

I've learnt and want to just say also, hard times don't last, good times do.

And if I was to fill out that booklet now with a list of things about myself I'd say:

1. I'm An Entrepreneur
2. I'm A Music Artist
3. I'm An Entertainer
4. I have my own TV show
5. I'm A Petrol Head
6. I'm A Dad

Gratitude And Peace

MARIAH IDRISSI

Model and humanitarian

When feeling overwhelmed with life, our human nature kicks in to fight or flight mode and it's our choice whether we rise above it or fall. Working for almost a decade in the fashion and entertainment industry has shown me how often I become overwhelmed with juggling it all, but it's also shown me how I deal with it. One thing that is so integral when working with people in business is not their accolades, network or years of experience but, in fact, it's their character we should pay great attention to.

Character development is a lifelong pursuit. We have all experienced some form of trauma or loss as well as joy and blessings. What matters not is what life throws at us but how we respond to it in order to heal, learn and grow. My spiritual path began with Islam and by the grace of God it ends that way too. Regardless of your faith or background, I believe we all need something that our lives revolve around. For me it's God but for others it could be money, their children or their hobbies. Whatever it is you centre your life around essentially becomes your religion and, for me, nothing is worthy of being centred around other than the One who created us.

That being said, in order to navigate my life I centre it around spiritual growth and that allows me to be more decisive and have clear goals. We all get distracted, it's human nature, but to pursue our distractions without catching ourselves is where things start to get messy. The same way we organise other areas of our life, we must also make spiritual growth or, as it's known in Islam, *tazkiya*, something we also organise in our lives too.

I was on a flight coming back to London from Morocco and contemplating the concept of *tazkiya*. As there was no wifi for me to do some research, I used the dying art of critical thinking and came up with my '7 steps to spiritual elevation'.

1. **Intention**
   We all have healing to do and for me that starts with the intention. The first step to anything we do with purpose should be intentional and sincere.

2. **Repentance**
   None of us are perfect. Often people hold themselves back from feeling worthy to ask for help because of their guilt, regret and ultimately sins. We are all worthy of God's mercy and encouraged to constantly turn back to Him with hope and confidence. Sincere repentance is a form of healing and redemption to put you in a mindset that allows you to forgive yourself and remove blockages to receive blessings.

3. **Acceptance**
   Faith to have hope and trust and keep moving forward without dwelling on the past once we have made amends with it.

4. **Supplication**
   Once you feel emancipated from the chains of guilt, regret and worry, supplication should feel easier because

both heart and mind are open and confident to simply ask. For many of us, there is a taboo around asking others for help, and that's an area I need to work on too!

5. **Gratitude**

There is a feeling of relief and tranquillity in knowing that, even if your external condition hasn't changed, internally you have made conscious actions towards positive change and healing within yourself. Discussing the gravities of gratitude is an entire book in itself, but being grateful is something we are all familiar with.

Gratitude for me has been a great form of healing, especially in times of grief and when things become overwhelming. It makes a world of difference to acknowledge that everything we experience is temporary. Rather than allowing the negative experiences to overshadow our lives, focus on nurturing and growing the good that is present.

6. **Servitude**

The most noble of people are those who serve others, in my humble opinion. Service to people and our planet is a form of service to God. It feels natural when in a state of gratitude to want to give to others and share that same feeling. Positive energy fuels life, the feeling of living and not just surviving. Outside of my public work, my humanitarian work is not just benefiting those on the other end but it benefits me in a magnitude of ways.

7. **Communication**

Communication is what makes us human. The ability to communicate with each other and also with our Creator.

Spiritually healing and having that clarity enables us to articulate our thoughts better as well as listen better. In order to respond, we must listen. It's often challenging to listen to the messages around us when the noise in our head is overpowering. It's no coincidence prophets, saints and the like have historically sought after a quiet space, whether it's on a mountain or in a cave, to find solitude and quietness.

A part of healing that I've recently begun to incorporate and want to include is creating your own reward system. Our world is a busy place so often we have to set time aside to reward ourselves, which I feel is a display of gratitude to The Most High for creating opportunities for us. Healing may not happen overnight but the process is something we should all work towards.

Hey God

M.MUSE

Writer and friend

Hey God,

It's me again. We have been on quite the ride for the last
couple of years; you have seen me through moments that I
didn't think that I could get past. Moments where you had to
send angels to pick me up from the floor and pour life into me;
moments where I cried so much that my eyes stung, and my
chest clung to the desperation of ending my pain. And just
when I thought I couldn't take any more, little pieces of hope
would settle themselves in the core of my chest, sometimes
shards from other people's joy or simply the energy to get out
of bed, but in those moments there was hope and light was
welcomed in. In those moments I was reminded that if I was
destined to drown, it would have happened already. I was
reminded that I was meant to be here, that my peace was
coming, I just had to hold on to those little pieces of hope. And
now I am. I am here, learning to live for the first time. I have
been blessed with a new start; trusting entirely in where my
soul is being called to. I want to thank you and my angels for
guiding me, protecting me, speaking life into me directly or
through others; for seeing that I was ready to live life as I
deserved to. I thank you.

I want to thank myself for giving in to the guidance that you
placed into me, for allowing myself to see my life, my past, my

choices – good and bad – for what they were, and not letting
what shined back at me make me retreat completely, instead
allowing it to push me to make the decisions that I always
knew I needed to make. I thank myself for turning inwards
where seeking external validation would have been easier. I
thank myself for letting go of things, spaces and people that are
not in tune with this new life that I am cultivating for myself. I
thank myself for not allowing my need for control to see me
return to old habits that bathed me in comfort but drowned me
in the end. I thank myself for the compassion that I am
showering myself in on the harder days. I thank myself for
connecting to my inner children and divine guidance. More
than anything, I thank myself for learning how to be a friend
to every part of who I have been, am and will be; I am learning
to love and treat them beautifully, as I learn to love all of me. I
have been through so much, and I can say that I am grateful
for the person that I see looking back at me. I couldn't see it
before, but every single version of me that had to live through
the unthinkable got me here; every painful event, every
moment of laughter, every moment of forced solitude – it was
all so that I could be here learning how to breathe again and
starting a life that celebrates me.

I didn't see life past thirteen, I hadn't planned to be here for
twenty-four, I couldn't see a future, so every birthday that came
was a surprise for me and I know that that has caused a lot of
difficulty for me; I have had to unearth and reintroduce myself
to the dreams I once had and see if they were still fitting for
who I have become, and I have found that they are. Each one
kissed my cheek as I unearthed them and gave them the
chance to breathe and unravel in front of me. This desire to
spend my life writing and creating hasn't left me; it was
divinely placed and there is no way to escape it, it is mine. I

know I was meant to find purpose in my pain, that is why I know pain so personally. I spent years desperate for other people's approval of my decisions and feelings. I think I had convinced myself that if someone told me that it was okay, then they would be valid, but I have learnt that I cannot live my life based on the co-signing of people who are also trying to figure life out. We are all just doing our best, and that is perfectly enough. As I step into this person that I am becoming, the world isn't small any more; my beliefs aren't limited to what people say is possible, I am learning to release myself from the chains of the beasts of my past. If I say that I want it, I trust that it is coming, and I walk through life with divine action of showing up for myself. I am letting it all happen for me. I don't need to be in control; life is so beautiful and so colourful; to control is to mute out colours because I am forcing myself to focus on what seems to suit me and the outcome I 'want'. Instead, I'm leaning into the fact that life is happening for me, so every colour, every laugh, every dream, every idea, every lesson, it all suits me perfectly.

God, you know that I am having moments when I don't know where I am going. It's like you put me in the ocean; you've given me this knowledge that there are millions of islands that are coming up and they are safe, abundant in everything that I need but I just have to keep on swimming forward, far away from the island that is behind me in clear view. You are telling me to let go of control and trust that all that I have requested is ahead of me even though I can't see it. I have that gut feeling that it's going to be okay but it doesn't stop the fear of not knowing what I'm doing. But I trust you and myself, so I am swimming forward. I know that as rough as some of the tides are in this ocean, the island behind me is not fruitful. I cannot plant or harvest in its soil. We are no longer compatible. I just ask that as I swim ahead, as I lean into faith and as I lean into myself – I ask that you continue to guide me, protect me, and fill me with light. Stay with me as I venture into this journey.

I have to keep reminding myself that I am deserving of this blessing. I won't lie, I have moments when my mind tries to return to what had been its home for so long. The space where I tell myself that I am not deserving of good things, the space that is decorated with unhealed wounds and beliefs that I am selfish for picking myself. It sometimes forgets that I burned that home. I think it still visits the rubble to protect itself. It fears that I might return there, but that is not our home any more. I have built this castle, a world of endless possibilities for it to roam amongst. I want to prove to my mind and inner child that they are safe with me again. That they can play, be childish, be silly, chase butterflies and dream without limitations – this new home is theirs to thrive within. I see them and myself so much clearer, I pick myself this time and every day beyond this moment.

I dedicate this new life to myself and all the versions of me that took the brunt of the lessons that came with getting here. I was so cruel to myself in the past, quick to punish myself for things I didn't know or wasn't equipped to deal with. I look back at my past selves with such a fondness. They picked up the pieces of themselves and shifted as life requested. They gave me the ability to be here. I promise to make them proud. To have my cheeks streak with tears of laughter, to allow myself to feel my feelings before they take over and become sinister, to check in with myself constantly and allow myself to see things for what they are, to be my own best friend and refuge. Life lives on my tongue, and I will speak it over myself. I am protected and loved; everything is going to work out for me. I will keep going, entering this new life of mine with childlike eyes, allowing myself to melt into the joy of the pinkest skies and the excitement of nature's blessings, to smile childishly at ideas that come to mind, moving fearlessly to make them happen. I am new to this, but I know that it is right for me because I am at peace. I am content. I don't have everything together, I don't need to; I have everything that I need, and I am stepping up as the person I have always wanted to be, I know that my blessings are running towards me.

I have come so far. These conversations used to be so much darker, and I would pray myself away, while asking you why I was still here. I want to thank you for not answering those prayers and instead surrounding me with love. You let me lash out, swear, throw things around (literally), scream and try to run away from myself, because you knew that I would always end up here. Receiving what was meant for me. It was just a matter of me being willing to receive it, to unlearn and trust. I know this is just the beginning, but I am so grateful for it. The last time I wanted to live, I was a child – so just waking up and feeling peace with that realisation is such a blessing. We got me here. We got me to twenty-four, with a new start and a heart that smiles. My inner child laughs so much and she's actually getting to be a child, she deserves this. It was all worth it. Thank You!

I know it's going to be magical.

Simple Things

PARIS CHONG

LEICA Gallery director, Los Angeles

Wishful, warning, wanting, wondering, blissful, hurting,
charming, daunting, feeling, fawning, needing, yawning,
seeing,
hearing, being sorry.

Listen to the simple things, listen when I call your name, hear
between the lines I say then maybe things will go our way.
Can't go on this road alone after knowing what I know.
Feel the taste of love in bed, hear the voice inside my head.
A scent, a touch, a glance, a sigh, makes me want to go inside
to be as one in a simple form, to make a choice, to make things
right to have the courage to make me right.

The Farewell Cuddle

MORRISSON

Rapper

Rest In Peace Stephen Morrisson

Growing up as four brothers and one sister, we'd argue and fight as all siblings would all the time. And there was a period where I hadn't seen my brother Stevo for a short while. A week before Father's Day 2020, I messaged him to meet.

He came to my house, pulled up in the drive, music blaring, banging on my door. I told him to keep the noise down and meet me in the park around the corner. Just me and him. We walked around the park for two hours, we cleared the air, we got everything off our chests, we spoke about our childhood, about our lives, everything we have been through and why we felt underappreciated by each other.

We covered everything and I told him I was going to help him with music and I was going to pay for rehab, I also told him, you're powerful and capable. When you go rehab, you're going to come out and I'm going to help you get a record deal, he's a good artist, he's an entertainer, he's more for the camera than I am. We laughed and joked together, all the stuff that had bothered us in the past had gone and we were brothers again.

The day I went to see my dad, it was Father's Day and I went over to his house and Stevo was there on a mad one and we were having a little catch-up, having a laugh and joke, getting along really well. He's winding my dad up, he took my phone and started filming all of us together. He said, let's write a card together for Dad and he was still filming. He recorded the whole thing and he gave the phone back and he said he's going to go now and he gave me a cuddle that felt like a farewell cuddle. I didn't like it, I didn't understand. It felt different to any other time before. As someone who is very spiritual and in tune, I still question why I didn't say something, but at the same time I didn't want to say it and put them thoughts into the universe.

A day or two later Stevo's life was sadly taken.

He was excited about music, we spoke about everything, about our childhood, the good and the bad, his ideas and what he wants to do. He wanted us to buy land and get a house with gates to get away from the world that tried to hurt us.

I used to tell him, 'That's never going to happen, all we'd do is argue.' He'd say, 'Trust me, John, we'll get all the bikes in there, and shut ourselves off from the world, away from the matrix.'

Back to that moment in the park, we was in a field with trees, there was no one listening, just us and nature. He had his pack of Haribo with him, he always had his pack Haribos, we came to an agreement regarding his future, 'Wicked idea, John,' he said. Later that evening he called me on FaceTime, and made us sing a song together, it was the theme song from Fifa that was on repeat from when we were kids and he told me to sing it with him, together on FaceTime, one of the lyrics being 'It wasn't easy'.

As sad as it is, I'm happy I got to make peace with my brother. If it wasn't for that, I don't think I'd be strong enough to make it through. It made the grieving process that little bit easier.

The World Outside Of YouTube

KSI

YouTuber

I look back at my younger self and cringe. Everybody does, but I have had more opportunities than others. Most of my life since my mid-teens is on YouTube – the good, the bad and the ridiculous. I leave it all up there because all of it has made me the man I am today – a thirty-year-old who knows how much he still has to learn.

When I started on YouTube, I had zero ambition. I was a lost, shy, introverted kid, feeling pressure from my parents to get a good job like a lawyer or an engineer. I didn't think I was smart enough and I knew I wouldn't enjoy it.

That changed when I reached a million subscribers, which was almost unheard of back then. It was a huge goal for me and is still the most important achievement of my life. It solidified my hard work. It made it real. The plaque is the first thing you see when you come into my home. Getting it told me I was worth something, that I had finally found my path.

For years I lived in an online bubble. Film, edit, post entertaining content, build up my subscribers. Rinse and repeat, rinse and repeat, rinse, and repeat. It was such a whirlwind that I didn't once stop to think about being a role model. I didn't realise the responsibility that came with my platform.

It was only when I first received a backlash in 2013, when the press began writing about me in a negative way, that I realised there is an outside world. It wasn't just my audience watching. It wasn't only people who spend their time on social media. YouTube is worldwide. Everyone can see it and I had to be aware of that.

When I made that first major mistake, I reacted as I imagine most kids would – I panicked. I only thought about myself. I worried that my whole career was over, that my hard work had come to nothing, that no one would want to watch me again.

Did I learn from my mistake? I like to think so, but this year, 2023, a decade on, I messed up again. I really upset the Pakistani community in a video by using an inappropriate slur. When the incident happened, I started to see that I was getting backlash and the South Asian community were upset with what I said. I was confused. I didn't truly understand the ramifications. I then became worried and after that I was just trying to figure out how to better the situation.

I don't excuse myself at all. I deeply regret it. The difference was that my first reaction was to take time out to understand the situation, educate myself and hold myself to account. I apologised, deleted the video, but I knew I had to do more to show how sorry I truly am.

In the months since, I've learnt so much about South Asian cultures and communities. Hussain reached out and we spoke straight away. He told me about the origins of the word and how it has affected him, the people in his life growing up and why so many people were upset by what happened. I learnt about the history of the word, the impact, the way people would be attacked and that slur be used against them and I knew to never say it again.

That was the start of my journey to heal the rift with the people I offended.

I went to a mosque in Bradford to talk to an imam, who was so welcoming and told me I'd messed up. I met a lot of people who love what I do and were disappointed in me. To see that disappointment on their faces really hit home. I also then found that there was a lot of educating that needed to happen, as outside of the UK I was noticing people were commenting saying they didn't understand the backlash of the term.

I went to the Kick It Out racism charity headquarters and met a young man called Raj, who agreed to give me a presentation about the racism he faced and the impact it had. He'd said he'd experienced racism his whole life. When he used to play football, his coach didn't care that he was being verbally abused by the opposition. He had no one to talk to and fell out of love with football because of it. I was angered hearing what he had been put through on purpose. The thought that I could have that negative impact on other people was devastating. I also visited a gurdwara in Kent and talked to a Sikh community leader. I've been to schools to tell my story and to charities to help. I have put everything in place to make sure I understand this word and am able to pass my new knowledge on.

In my YouTube videos, I talk about everything that happens in my life. I go on social media and chat to fans. Being the person who can educate them is my positive. I'm using my platform for good.

I've never pretended to be perfect, someone who never makes mistakes. That wouldn't be relatable. Everyone messes up sometimes. I've done a lot of crazy things, a lot of great things and my fair share of stupid things. Together, they have shaped the person I am now.

I look back at myself as a teen and realise I didn't understand how the real world worked. I understood my

YouTube bubble and I thought that was enough. I was terrified of talking in public, but as soon as the camera turned on I put on an act and was able to perform.

Now I'm much more myself. I'm comfortable in my own skin. Boxing has given me so much mental strength. It's made me realise I can do things I never thought I was capable of, not only in the ring. It's not success that makes me feel powerful – it's knowing that I am in control of my life, that I'm learning and becoming a better man. My audience has been with me throughout that journey and seen me mature. I'm grateful to have them with me.

I've always hated the term influencer. Everyone on this Earth is an influencer – we all influence the people around us, in lots of different ways. It's how you use your influence that matters.

What's next? I want to start a family. It would be lovely to have kids to show them all sides of life and pass down what I have learnt as a father. I'd be an up-to-date dad, definitely.

Meanwhile, I'll continue to work hard and use the position I've been given to help. I'm at a point in my career where I want to give back. I have done a lot of entertaining for audiences. Now I have the money and the influence to make a difference. I've started a record label and a platform for putting on fights to help people follow me into both music and boxing. Mental health charities are another priority for me.

I love seeing other people succeed. I feel real pride in having helped them. I love jumping on other YouTubers and seeing success spread to those who deserve it. I believe that if you put out good karma, it comes back in the end.

I'll be eternally sorry for the hurt and upset that my

comment caused and eternally grateful to all of the people who helped me start the healing.

I'll still be online, but I prefer to be present in the real world these days, aware that I have so much still to discover.

Be Careful What You Wish For Son

OLLY WILLIAMS

Artist, poet and friend

For Bear and Kora

'So, you want to be an artist?' the balding tutor asked.

'Yes,' I said. 'I do.'

'So, tell me about you?'

'I'm a rugby player, or I was, until recently . . .', I managed to blurt. Ear bitten off, back fucked, sorry, hurt. Guess I've always had the two things going on.

'What two things?' the interviewer asked, intrigued.

'The creative/destructive thing.'

The panel concurred, hushed tones.

'You look like you could move heavy desks and screens?' Baldy pointed. I followed his long finger, across my portfolio, to a stack of partitions on wheels in the corner of the studio.

'No problem,' I answered. 'Happy to help shift anything.' More knowing smirks. And that was it. A place on the degree course at Central Saint Martins landed unceremoniously – brown letter, second class stamp – a week later. Thirty-five years on, I sometimes meditate on this conversation. What if I had not belligerently stuck it out, met Suzi, gone off grid into the wild? Missed the groovy art party swelling around us . . . and missed all the magnificent creatures we have met; Fitzy, Robert, monumental mentors, all we had seen and learnt of wilderness. What we had pitched and lost back home; failed at, struggled to overcome. The lack of perceived security; homeless, pensionless, penniless. But at fifty-five, a dad still grafting; inspired, engaged, strangely happy. Proud of my kids, my wife. My chosen life. Be careful what you wish for son, for you alone must live with the companionship of your decisions.

Time Will Fly

SAM TOMPKINS

Singer-songwriter

You're gonna meet some new friends
But one'll die
Then you're gonna be depressed
And that's fine
You may even find love
A few times
Then you're gonna break up
But that's life

You're out weekly
Now you're on sixteen
On ship street
Working on a big dream
To make an EP
And throw it on a CD
Then radio
On repeat

You were right
You did everything that you said you would do
So don't try
To give it up that's what they want you to do

Time will fly
Run away from you
And it's right
It's what you're made to do
You will cry
But that's what's taken you
To one whole night
Where you don't have pain in you

You're gonna meet your hero
you know the guy
Yeah, you're gonna go far
That high
People will sell you dreams
Enough times
But you'll read the TCs
And dotted lines

You know why
You're playing those strings
In the morning 'til the
Late night,
Putting in work
'Cause it's all you knew

Time will fly
Run away from you
And it's right
It's what you're made to do
You will cry
But that's what's taken you
To one whole night
Where you don't have pain in you

I think it's a shame that you can't talk to your younger self
cause a lot of the times when I was younger I needed someone
    exactly like me to show up and be there when I needed
    them . . .
But, I'm there for them now

Time will fly

Run away from you

And it's right

It's what you're made to do

You will cry

But that's what's taken you

To one whole night

Where you don't have pain in you

Little Did I Know, I Deserved Love

FREDDIE PEARSON

Actor, dear friend

As a naive, thrill-seeking eighteen-year-old, the world of modelling seemed like any teenage boy's dream. Female attention, fancy clothes, luxurious holidays, free gifts and even the jealousy of other boys fuelled my fire.

But as I began my course as a student at Manchester University, I ran into some trouble. Having grown up in the hustle-bustle lifestyle of London and the ambitious, hard-working nature of my parents, I found it incredibly difficult to switch off. I began to use my free time to focus on modelling; to reach out to photographers and companies, brands and directors to try to create opportunities for myself. I tried to mould my image off successful people in my industry and compared them to those around me. I tried to control the uncontrollable.

After a strict diet with a prominent figure in the photography world, and the obsession with this career path, I began to crumble. An eating disorder, six-hour-plus Instagram days, continuous comparison and an obsession with my image reduced me to my knees. I wanted to quit modelling on so many occasions. I felt devalued, diminished and unconfident in my own skin; my confidence had turned to insecurity. I hadn't booked a job in over a year, and I felt useless at the one thing I had believed in myself for; how could I go from being confident and self-assured from my external image to not even recognising myself in the mirror?

I had judged, evaluated and compared myself, as I felt those around me had. I didn't feel anything positive towards my own image. Until I realised that everything I was feeling were the thoughts, anxieties and projections from other people's opinions. How had I let the noise of the external world have such a profound effect on my own opinion of myself? How had I allowed the rejection of one industry to make me feel completely inadequate?

So why didn't I quit? Why didn't I walk away from such a brutal industry? I had faced rejection at every corner, I had compared myself to the point of no value and I had thrown all my eggs in one basket, only for them to be shattered.

I didn't quit because I realised that I had so much more to offer to the world than my vanity had originally taught me. I realised that the brutality of such an industry was a free education looking me in the face. Lessons about the nature of the world around me, the sacrifices made for success and who I am really. What really lies behind those blue eyes and what can I learn?

I learnt to value myself for my character. I learnt to appreciate my mind, and not just my body. I started being kinder to myself, and less obsessive about my image. I learnt to not take things so personally and to stand up for myself regardless of others' opinions. I wanted to quit, but I didn't – and it's made me so much stronger for it.

However, looking back at my experiences in the modelling industry, there is a bigger lesson I've learnt and something I've come to understand. Just because you've come from a place of pain, if you've experienced trauma or if you've ever felt suffocated in your grief, it doesn't mean you have to stay there – that does not have to become the story of your life; it is possible to turn a page and to start a new chapter.

Throughout my adolescence, and especially when I was modelling, I felt very on my own. I felt isolated and, at times, no good to this world. I didn't fit in that well, and I would often feel incredibly lonely and question myself. For a long time, I believed that was how the rest of my life would be.

I healed because I knocked the idea that 'being selfish' was a negative thing on the head; I decided to change the way I saw myself by changing the way I viewed the world around me. I decided that being an outsider didn't have to be a lonely thing – instead, why not let it liberate me? Instead of trying to fit in, why not stand out and see my value without feeling the need for approval?

When we are very young, we are always taught that being selfish is a negative thing – and actually, being selfish and putting yourself first is not only necessary, but vital to your survival and happiness. Only after you accept and love yourself will you find yourself in a place and position to accept and love other people.

You deserve good things in your life. You deserve to experience wonderful things that make you believe in good in this world. You are not the mistakes you once made, the pain you once experienced or the rejection you've faced. You are a vessel that deserves to be overflowed and filled with joy. You deserve love in your life and bandages for your wounds.

You deserve love.

Let Me Be

EBONEE DAVIS

American model, poet, actor, author
and founder of daughter.org

I wish to be removed
From the pedestal of perfection
To fall to break to crumble
To trip to snare to stumble
To bear the weight of my imperfection
Without expectation
Imagine plummeting to the ground
With scorched wings
And being told
To 'just fly'
I would like my pain to be visible
To the eye
In the same way
My strength seems to be
Do you recognise
What has injured me?
Because I am in an unfamiliar hell
With a pain I have never felt
So please let me feel it
Let me grow accustomed
To knowing the shape of it
Let me, at least, learn to live with it
And, at best, to love it
I am still your superwoman

Not because I am invincible
But because I make visible
My scars
For the world to see
Even when I am broken
I still give the pieces
So let me be
Do not tell me to be strong
I was that before the pain
Do not remind me of my greatness
Right now I want to be weak
I do not want to pick myself up
By the bootstraps
I have spent my life
Doing that
And I am exhausted
I do not want to seal the cracks
I am okay with falling apart
And I am okay with the idea
That what comes next
Is not art
It does not have to be beautiful
Ugly holds value too
I am okay with my location
So ask yourself
Why you so badly
Need me to move?

Artist Statement
It's worth observing how compassionless people can become
towards the very individuals they admire most. How quickly
pain is dismissed or minimised when people perceive you as

strong. Even if offered earnestly, 'if anybody can get through it, it's you' feels more like a dagger than a pillow. Why are we so eager to rush those suffering out of their pain, instead of holding space for it, as if their discomfort will spill onto us? Even our own inner voices can be critical in this way.

It is true that one should not spend their entire lives traversing and replaying the trauma they've endured. However, emotions are intelligence too. They carry with them wisdom worth exploring and extracting. They also occupy space. And if we do not feel them, face them and experience them in their entirety, they will take up permanent residence in the vessels we inhabit.

We must start to think of emotions as objects with mass and volume rather than inconvenient abstractions. We can hold them, study them and let them go. And there is no part of that process that should bring us fear or that we should skip over for the sake of keeping to all together.

Keep Your Spirit Strong – A Conversation
JOHN BURTON

Lighthouse keeper

A text message conversation

HUSSAIN: Can't believe I'm taking the risk and leap of
faith.

UNCLE JOHN: I can. You are stronger than you believe.

HUSSAIN: Thank you for everything.

HUSSAIN: I know you don't pray.

HUSSAIN: But do wish me well.

HUSSAIN: I have no idea what I am doing.

UNCLE JOHN: Yes I wish you well. And in my way I pray for
you. Will be more of a spiritual resonance with me thinking
positively about you. Unreligous praying.

HUSSAIN: Uncle John

HUSSAIN: Hope ur ok

HUSSAIN: What advice would you give me on my last day of
being 31? x

UNCLE JOHN: Wow, what a question. I say, 'don't look back with regret, jealousy or negativity; watch what you eat (your metabolism may slow down??); and keep working hard; as you are still SO YOUNG'.

Also keep your spirit strong

HUSSAIN: Can I get some advice

UNCLE JOHN: Sure, what's the question?

HUSSAIN: Am I doing okay in life?

UNCLE JOHN: Wow that's a complicated question. We all have lots of facets. Some can be great while others not so great or even bad. So in reality none of us are doing ok across every single facet. There are people I like aspects of, but I will not trust information.

I think you are doing really well in going on your chosen path without any support or road map. You have parts of your character that are still confused about that choice e.g. the strong cultural and religious emphasis on the importance of say getting married and having kids is one example.

I think you have chosen a hard road, but that it's the right and correct road for you, which is admirable, but inevitably there are parts of your life you need to alter or leave behind.

You want to talk later?

HUSSAIN: I have so much appreciation for u

HUSSAIN: Lovely photo, we look happy and the box is full of love

UNCLE JOHN: I am very proud to be able to call you a friend. Seems like you might be on the cusp of another change. Go with it and don't over worry about it as your life will probably change. But I don't think you will ever lose or forget your roots

HUSSAIN: Thank you so much

HUSSAIN: Stay close to me

HUSSAIN: I am very proud of you too

HUSSAIN: You teach me a lot about life and how to be a better man / person

UNCLE JOHN: For sure. I will always be here for you. But if you need time dedicated to the new road, I get that too

HUSSAIN: No none of this please

HUSSAIN: Thank you ☺

UNCLE JOHN: Okay, sleep well

John Burton
Following the themes of the book . . . I call myself an 'optimistic pessimist'. I have hope but with a heavy dose of reality thrown in. I cannot lean on religion as I am not a believer. I put my faith in what we can do on this planet (even though there are too many humans not practising humanity or acting with respect and civility). I am no perfectionist. I am more of a bodger and do not overly worry in seeing

imperfections in my activities – although I do try my hardest to get the best results I can.

Health: for me that's about regular exercise but not fitness. It's about having mind and body linked and the journey to get there. On reflection a lot of my activities allow me to do several things within each one. Exercise is vital. Walking is really important, but, more so, I have been cycling to and from work for forty-five years now and have been learning tai chi for the last nineteen years (wish I had started earlier – tai chi is a very long road).

Hustle: my hustle is not about bending morality or about the search for riches. It is about keeping going and keeping from overreacting to things. I try to keep calm wherever possible (not easy, folks). I work where various shades are needed, not always binary decisions. I do not remember a point in time when having the attitude to just get on with things became part of me. I was lucky enough to be encouraged that way and to see that we are always learning. My mind is open to listening to different views and I try not to judge people from first impressions. My attitude is to be open to who people are. Also I am very methodical which ensures I tackle things from the start and do not jump in at the deep end. Sounds nice and simple, but this quality is so important. Many folks I know do not follow it, so often my contribution is to bring people together and start from the beginning.

Help: so far I have not looked for therapy as in the context of this book I do not need it. But I have had help in all sorts of ways over my life from all sorts of folks, including my wife, children, friends, work and education colleagues.

Healing: I work on looking after my body and mind. My life is imperfect, but one area I can relax about is that I know I will keep going, plugging away and not feeling bad because results do not come fast or in the way I hoped for. Making things with your hands is so important too. I was lucky to grow up in a creative family. Music was really present, as was learning craft and DIY skills.

While I did not follow that as a career (I work for Hussain's landlord and he came to me looking for a studio to work from), the ethos of having a range of pastimes or hobbies has been a constant in my life.

Finally, I am old enough not to be dominated by social media. I turn off all notifications, which is a great way to keep myself to myself.

Loving Me, Again

MAX BOWDEN

Father, actor, friend

Yesterday was the most perfect time spent with my son and I couldn't be more grateful. Across the board – mature conversation between two co-parents.

I'm grateful for my parents and how much they bring to my son's life. I'm grateful for sobriety and clarity.

I'm grateful for innovation and good ideas, I'm reaping the rewards of sobriety and the changes.

I am drawing myself to make business decisions I'm proud of.

Grateful for my time at *EastEnders* and that it's coming to a close.

Grateful for that first cup of tea.

I am grateful for having doors opened.

I'm grateful to be of good health both mentally and physically.

Grateful for the love I'm being shown and am giving in many different directions.

I'm grateful for expansion and my friend Hussain who grows everything alongside me and I have neglected that relationship for a while, so I'm extra grateful for him today!

I'm grateful for creativity again, allowing my mind time to digest, yet work overtime when I require it.

I'm grateful for ADHD; it allows me so much thinking space.

I'm grateful for good relationships, peace of mind, internal clarity, and a true knowledge of how I am feeling about myself.

Grateful for the ability to love me again.

Stay With Me

SARAH CALLAGHAN

Poet

I never know how to start these things so I'll begin by saying I
    don't have the answers.
None of us do.
But I know darkness.
And I know pain.
I know frustration, regret, shame and sadness.
Bones made of metal weighing you down onto the bed making
    it impossible to rise from the slumber.
Guilty; thinking I'm not doing enough.
I'm not enough.
I don't have a university degree
And I don't know what some big words mean
But I know feelings.
I understand how you feel when you give me that look.
I read people like books.
We all search for answers
For meanings
When sometimes the meaning is, there isn't one.
Goals divide the year up nicely
Deadlines and dreams theoretically mapped out over our
    lifetimes
Which hold so much pressure.
When we don't achieve, which happens, it comes crashing
    down on you like a tsunami breaking hearts,

Chipping away at our self-esteem,
And slowly we drown.
Stay with me.
Stay with me.
Stay with me.
We must learn to navigate our way through these choppy
    waters.
Don't hold on to dreams so tightly that it makes your fist sore.
Same with people.
Adore them but give them freedom.
Give yourself freedom too.
The art of finding balance between working towards an
    amazing future and enjoying the present is difficult.
But not impossible.
The future may never come.
So what are you working for?
What are you trying to achieve if every moment of magic, right
    here, is missed?
Picking all the fruits leaves a tree bare.
You get me?
The constant cycles of despair
I know all that.
But because I know darkness, I know light.
Because I know sadness, I know joy.
Disappointment, excitement.
Depression, elation.
Tears and being so gassssssed I have to spell it with bare S's
    and a million emojis.
I don't know much but I know these times won't last forever.
I know storms pass.
I know people care about you more than you think.
Never lose hope, it is the greatest gift you have.

Love is endless so give it away in huge portions – it will keep
  refilling until you take your last breath and I promise when
  you die you won't have any regrets.

The beauty of life is that we are everything and nothing.
Don't you understand?
None of it matters while every day is a miracle
Duality forever bringing us back round to where we started.
Right here.
In this moment.
How amazing is that?
You are doing great.
You are doing just, great.
Ignore society's expectations and make your own meanings.
Every day is precious.
So, make it a priority to strive to see it.
And when you do,
Let me know what it's like.

Healing Waves

MEGGAN ROXANNE

Founder of TheGoodQuote & author of How To Stop Breaking
Your Own Heart

If it's true what they say
That healing comes in waves
Then am I supposed to go through life keeping my guards up
    and anticipating the day,
Where anxiety and fear resurfaces its face
or is there ever going to be a time on this journey where I can
    relax and feel safe?

Coz I just made it back to shore
After the last hurricane
And the pain I overcame simply ensured
that I'm not coming back as who I was before coz my heart's
    not the same,

And to be honest, after years of living in the comfort zone
    where I tried my best to remain,
I'm surprised my efforts brought to me a place where I'm
    finally at peace and now I'm just trying to maintain,

So be honest with me?

Is this place of grace, where my soul finds ease, somewhere I
    can stay. Coz I just want to feel at home again and yes I have
    faith when I pray, but I can't help but fear the possibilities of

being on this road again, and maybe you can say that I'm
frightened of change, but I'm trying my best not to lose hope
again,

So be honest with me?

How do I find balance in this space?

And it's mad that I'm asking these questions as I stand face to
  face with the answers. Because as I walked through the
  trenches of trauma, the strength within me was already
  planted, and set in a place, which reminded me that
  turbulent waves are meant to be embraced, because that's
  the location where our resilience is traced,

See it's all on purpose, healing can't be rushed so slow down
  your chase, coz in this life it's the norm, you have to pass
  through the storm, and be patient and wait, let the waves
  find its own pace, and trust that its waters will peacefully
  drift you towards the serene shores of a lake.
But in the meantime, Meg, you're safe.

Your Smile Is Brighter Than The Sun
SAIDA AHMED

Actress, writer, friend

Your smile is brighter than the sun.
Did you know that your smile sets you apart from everybody
    else?
Even if you smile for just a little while,
You might be encouraging everyone else around you to start
    smiling themselves,
Even if you may not be feeling like yourself.

Your smile is brighter than the sun,
Your smile is second to none,
Your smile is your superpower,
So why don't you use it more?
Your smile is brighter than the sun
So why are you frowning for?

Did you know that smiling is considered a charity?
Your smile is brighter than the sun
Your smile brightens up your face
Your smile adds clarity to your personality,
Let alone your face.

Your smile is brighter than the sun,
But I'm not here to tell you what to do,
Smile because you want to,

Not because you have to,
Your smile is brighter than the sun
So take your time,
And smile at your own time,
Because you're in control of your own happiness,
So smile whenever you want to,
It's totally up to you,
What you wish to do.

Your Friend In The Middle Of The Night

HUSSAIN MANAWER

Hot sweats
Panting breaths
Can't sleep
Falling deep
It doesn't feel nice

The furthest from alright
Trauma rings through the body
Ringing of the universes sensitive satellites
Now i'm sleeping on top of my sheets
To avoid falling into the darkness
Through dreams
I lay here wishing for a touch
But all i find is me in my mind stuck in the mud, deep in a
ruck, wanting to give up

Another episode
Another night
Another chance
But i'm trying to view this as another chance
For me to get it right

Hey, I'm glad you're awake. Means I don't have to sit through this weird funk of an episode by myself

- It's okay, I really get it, look you have been through a lot and trauma is actually stored in the body

What really?

- Yeah, it is, so when you start working on your body it begins to exercise your muscles and work through what you have been going through, but sometimes it still can knock you off guard

Tell me about it

- No, why don't you tell me about it

Okay I will, I spend so much time with my close friends and keep so much of my past hurt away from them, because I don't want to burden them with my life problems and such, so i internalise everything. Even around people I love, I guess this then shows in different ways in my behaviour that doesn't really seem to be 'normal'.

- Why do you keep it from them?

Well, because I used to be the funny guy, not the everything is so deep, I then start thinking maybe I am actually just an attention seeker and I don't want to work through anything. I just want their attention and then get upset when I don't get it

- Buddy, don't let your mind play this trick on you, you have gone through so much you deserve to speak about it as much or as little as you want especially with your close friends, that doesn't make you an attention seeker, if anything it's noble of you to do it

Really?

- Yes, really, don't keep things bottled up inside you, you're a human being before anything else and you have to express these things, like you are doing here tonight. Because in expressing these emotions do you know what you realise

No, what?

- You really are not by yourself, you are not alone and even though I am so far away from you right now I just want you to know I love you, see these words as the biggest hug, and I will sit with you through this one, so I'm kinda glad your trauma woke you up this evening

Really, why's that?

- Because it means me and you got to spend some wonderful bonding time together, how often is it you get to hear from your past self and future self in one piece?

Yeah that's pretty something, we've never done this before have we Hussain?

- Na never bro, well done for showing up for yourself

Thanks man, I think I'm going to try go back to sleep now

- Good night and remember, it's okay, you're doing
  wonderful and everything you are processing and
  experiencing is completely natural, you're not missing out
  on anything in life, you are doing absolutely wonderful,
  okay?

Okay

- Say it like you mean it

Yeah okay! I got you, I feel you and I believe you

- Great, goodnight champ, I'm so proud of you x

Feeling lighter
Oh the blessings of being a midnight writer
Sometimes it's ok to continue to be the one in the story who
stays being the fighter
Stay still if you need to, before you take it any higher

Don't burn yourself but find a way to embrace the fire
It's beautiful

You letting your emotions out and being a cryer
Try to view the situation as being delicate
Instead of viewing the situation as being dire
Your living life through your sentences well,
Bless yourself, for always being a tryer

There's no rule book compatible
Between the mania and the magical
Not every solution to your emotional needs at this stage is
tangible
But all of what could explode is by default flammable
Which isn't always fair
But that be life
So before you leave and wonder back into your sleep in the
middle of the night
I'm not going to say everything will be alright

But you know what it might be,
A little less heavy, a little more light,
A little bit of a push on the trajectory
In the middle of the turbulence of your flight

Baby boy, your doing more than fine
What you've experienced to how your handling it
Is graceful and for that, I know in my heart of hearts

You, genuinely will be alright x

The Final Word

ANDREA THOMPSON

Fashion designer & founder of WESTILLMOVE clothing brand

Somewhere deep down inside, I had told myself that I am not deserving of the things that I want in Life – it was the only reason why I did not have them.

It was only until I accepted and understood this, I automatically changed the narrative of my Life.

I am deserving of the things that I want in Life, and now knowing this, it will be the reason why I have them.

When self-belief is not in play, seeking validation is.

When validation is being met, all is well.

When validation is not being met, it is not.

So I tell you

The only validation you need is from God and then inevitably yourself.

To whoever is reading this, I tell you now you are so worthy of your dreams and more. If you can visualise it in your mind, then it is already done. Do whatever it is you have to do to bring it into your reality – but only with Love – and undoubtedly it shall be yours.

I owe it to the inner child, I owe it to me, I owe it to myself. I owe it to her.

If I can change just one Life with WESTILLMOVE, then my job here is done. Until then, I cannot give up.

This is my reason Why. What is yours?

Signing Out
Andrea – WESTILLMOVE – Thompson

Thank You

Thank You, **Anonymous**
For penning your majestic words,
Full of wisdom, heart and understanding to be felt and heard
As the opening statement of this anthology

Thank You, **Anonymous**
For creating the Original Slam
That changed so many of our lives
One mic, one spotlight,
Clicks, away, forever, today
Much love dear friend, honestly x

Thank You, **Sinéad Harnett**
For illustrating that surrendering
Is self-advocating
That allows us to really embrace our dreams properly

Thank You, **Dame Til Wykes**
For gracing the start of the opening chapter
With mental health as the prime factor
Embedded with your knowledge and philosophy

Thank You, **Lola Young**
For 'T is For Trauma'

Your flow of poetic rhythm and order
Sharing a piece so personal from your psychology

Thank You, **Paula Naughton**
For showing us all
Love in all of its measures
Is within the chest of life and its treasures
That will forever be the strongest currency

Thank You, **Annika Waheed**
For taking us in to learn
Within the depths of hell week when it burns
From what you are dealing with in real time medically

Thank You, **Louise Hill-Davis**
For explaining your story, that proves
We can't stop now
There's so much to do
In the fight for equality in health policy

Thank You, **Ren Gill**
For sharing your experiences with Lyme disease and
psychosis
And how you found hope through constant misdiagnosis
With your powerful spirit, artistry and methodology

Thank You, **Niah Selway**
For demonstrating that resilience is brilliance
And with strong willpower just like you
We can break every single self-fulfilling prophecy

Thank You, **Larry Lamb**
For allowing us the intimate insight
To what you are experiencing personally in life
Openly and honestly

Thank You, **Kevin Hines**
For highlighting that we do not need to get
caught in our thoughts
They do not need to be become our actions,
most certainly

Thank You, **Anonymous**
For your candour and sincerity
I pray that love provides you security
Whilst loving you abundantly in all of its transparencies

Thank You, **Dan Dare**
For welcoming us into your heart
From a moment so heartbreakingly hard
And by so proving that talking is one of the greatest
therapies

Thank You, **Sonna Rele**
For your light, life, love and kindness
For your golden voice,
And incredible melodies

Thank You, **Surfing Sofas**
The bad hand could never overrule the pen and your plan
You are a blessing for our world, your penmanship
Your teachings and energies

Thank you, **Nick Jones**
For the importance and encouraging reinforcement
Around the lessons gained, that we may not see, but we must learn
Around the theme of 'succeeding'

Thank You, **AJ Wavy**
For showcasing
For trailblazing
The spirit and power of family, music & self-believing

Thank You, **Arnas Fedaravičius**
For taking us to the station at Tottenham Court Road
To stand beside the street performer
Who then revealed to us all, the vital lessons that life was teaching

Thank You, **Jake Wood**
For highlighting that we can never
Regardless of pressure
Or anything else in that matter
Quit dreaming

Thank You, **Corin Hardy**
For explaining how the wings of a butterfly
Can extend their reach beyond the skies
Once they elegantly glide beyond the glass ceiling

Thank You, **Corinna Brown**
For evidently showing
Determination will most certainly keep you growing
A word, valuable, powerful and pivotal

Thank You, **Micheal Ward**
For your powerful words, from your inspiring story
Thank you for encouraging us and showing us it's important to
follow your dreams
So that we can achieve the unpredictable

Thank You, **Glen Powell**
For presenting passion and spirit
When combined with ambition to show no limit
All being crucial human principles

Thank You, **Murray Cummings**
For reminding us to enjoy every step
To take a second to breathe and reflect
And to not just wait for the pinnacle

Thank You, **Michael Adex**
For delving into the hustler's mentality
Giving us the steps to follow, to develop actively
Through behaviour, habit and principle

Thank You, **Jay Ellis**
For breaking down what's achievable
Even when at times, it doesn't seem feasible
If we protect, adapt and most importantly stick to our
vision

Thank You, **Danny Ramirez**
For the personal and professional insight
To the inside of your life
Taking us through important decisions
Along with the importance of precise precision

Thank You, **Maryam Pasha**
For clarifying quitting,
Sometimes along the road
As hard as it maybe to accept,
Is what we might actually need to envision

Thank You, **Anonymous**
For educating us
On all obstacles you undeservingly
But yet so courageously face on your mission (*you got this*)

Thank You, **Kiran Sonia Sawar**
For your enlightening words
In this book and real life, have taught me work and worth
Thank you for taking us in to the wings on your mission

Thank You, **Maro Itoje**
For sharing with us the power of the mind
What it's capable when it thrives
and what it can achieve once it's made its decision

Thank You, **Tyler West**
For outlining and highlighting
Through every lesson we may be stressing
When deep down, there's actually a blessing

Thank You, **Colin Salmon**
For reminding us that breathing
And holding on,
Through second guessing,
Is progression

Thank You, **Courteney Cox**
For highlighting the need of replacing self deprecating
With positive thoughts and manifesting
As we develop through life and it's new phases

Thank You, **Misha B**
For your friendship and your powerful poem
'The Love Within'
It's flame truly sets alight this anthology's pages

Thank You, **Matt Eagles**
For your constant positivity
Your humour and humility
Through all of life and what it may present with its cases

Thank You, **James Smith**
It touches my heart,
You thanking your mum
Traveling the world with your music and art
As your writing bangers on countless pages

Thank You, **Zinnia Kumar**
For breaking boundaries
Replacing societal norms
Paving a way for a new generation
As we look towards where the stage is

Thank You, **Jack Harries**
For your efforts with me in Pakistan
And also presenting why it's important to realign
with our purpose
As we grow to new ages

Thank You, **Hamzah Sheeraz**
For your inspiration in and outside of the ring
Whilst elaborating on the power of hope,
And how so evidently
It can take us to all these new places

Thank You, **Bunmi Mojekwu**
For being inspirational to me from day one
With your work and in this book with your entry
Emphasising we should and must
Trust the signs from the universe,
As they appear when they are presented

Thank You, **Hero Fiennes Tiffin**
For detailing opposing viewpoints
Even when it doesn't make sense
Breaking away from how our thoughts were once
cemented

Thank You, **Ben Shephard**
For not listening and for detailing
The valuable lessons for us all to learn from
From what you have experienced through your career presenting

Thank You, **Jaspreet Kaur**
For sharing your poem, your name, your words
Allowing your work
To take us to a place where it's transcending

Thank You, **Ryan Adagio Winch**
For unpacking your pen,
Scribing life through your lens

Through fatherhood
Where love in all angles is deeply extending

Thank You, **Jeremy Vine**
For being the ray collector,
May the beams ignite the night
Filled with hope and love to never be ending

Thank You, **Ryan Keen**
For being on this journey of life with me,
The wonderful moments we've shared
And all the love and blessings that are coming
That are surely pending

Thank You, **Jordan Stephens**
For presenting there is always hope
Hidden in the notes,
For moments when we feel that may we not be able to cope
It has powers to be mending

Thank You, **Greg Tarzan Davis**
For installing in our frames of mind,
In your words
'We can't get tired
We don't get tired'
Thank you for all the incredible energy you're sending

Thank You, **Emma Hedile Al-Munshi**
For sharing the important piece; 'A Chameleon's Skin'
Within *I Wanted To Quit Too*,
Your words and friendship are a true blessing

Thank You, **Gian Power**
As resilience is a word you have redefined
With all the power that lies in your smile, they can never take,
Thank you for representing

Thank You, **Brady Campbell**
For sharing your story at the age of ten
For making that lemonade
For the bravery, love and hope you represent

Thank You, **Anonymous**
For allowing us to ensure your story is heard
Thank you, for sharing what causes so much hurt
The truth felt behind every single one of your words
Your voice we shall protect

Thank You, **Chidera Eggerue**
For making us promise to never give up,
Even on our darkest days
When we can't seem to find a way
Them words hold deep, as we take moments to reflect

Thank You, **Greg Williams**
For showing me,
Help is something we are never too old to get
For comfortingly confronting me,
In many ways I will forever hold and respect

Thank You, **Roger Streako King Tutu**
The mountain we climb, for real, holds many steps
Many moments of much needing healing
And lyrical and spiritual intellect

Many more blessings to collect

Thank You, **Joel Robison**
For your words, friendship and how you incredibly
Creatively interject,
Emails from you, are the best subjects,
Thank you, for always designing everything to be so perfect

Thank You, **Holly-Marie Cato**
For taking us on a journey
Detailing every cause and effect
For really highlighting the things that can help us
Are not always the things that we necessarily expect

Thank You, **Dhillan B**
For throwing it on to a t-shirt
For teaching me to embrace my inner mess
For showing me I deserve love
Can I get a - hell yes!

Thank You, **Fady Elsayed**
You taught me energy and frequency
The story of 'The Square'
Highlights humanity and it's decency
Thank you for showing us the importance of treating people equally

Thank You, **Natasha Ali**
I never understood, A Mother's Guilt
Until I read your powerful piece
And now I know,
I live everyday religiously

Thank You, **Kieron Boothe**
For being the artist, lyricist,
wordsmith and creative you are,
The colours of the city have taught me to protect
My own palette, in order to live peacefully

Thank You, **Kirsty Latoya**
For lending your powerful pen,
That's changed countless lives
And for your digital artistry that allows the mind to live
dreamily

Thank You, **Goody From Leeds**
For penning the words of your piece
Showcasing what they didn't teach
Didn't stop you, from finding and reaching
That stage of inner love and inner peace

Thank You, **Steel Banglez**
For being a true inspiration
Highlighting your depression
How you battled through it
With great musical succession
Your art is such a powerful much needed weapon

Thank You, **Lucrezia Millarini**
For highlighting the bond of a relationship with humans and
animals
It's something I never grew up understanding
But reading your piece I understand how this is needed for
progression

Thank You, **Bashir 'Double S' Bazanye**
For your beautiful piece on gratitude
A piece that allows our mind to freshen
It's compression, a much needed, healthy, daily
Confession

Thank You, **Obaidullah**
For allowing me to be a small part of your incredible journey
You unknowingly taught me and countless others
Many lessons

I pray you are reunited with your family x

To The People Of Pakistan, thank you for allowing us to help
Phir Milenge
(We Will Meet Again)

Thank You, **Doctor Poetry**
For giving us our first glance at The Rhythmic Ward
We can't wait to access your doors
And enter the Corridor of Chords

Thank You, **Nihal Arthanayake**
For penning such a powerful letter
That there are many ways we can strive to be better
Thank you for being a trailblazer, it's wonderful watching you soar

Thank You, **Lioness**
For 'The Shade I'm In', reading it over and over
Gave me multiple feelings
And I feel incredibly empowered approaching that final line
Because it's true, 'they can't break within'
I can't wait for your music and so much more

Thank You, **The Unwed Wife**
I can't even begin to think to imagine
How hard them words were to write
I'm grateful to you all, and i'm always here
You have a friend and brother for life
That I've sworn x

Thank You, **Harris J**
For explaining we are having to hurt to heal
Thank you my brother for sharing something so deeply to
what you feel
With what you deal and what you've worn
I love you my bro, forever more x

Thank You, **Mist**
For opening your heart
I'm inspired by your ability and capabilities
To create change, family, love
Through music, business and art
Whilst constantly opening doors

Thank You, **Mariah Idrissi**
For the stages of fight or flight
Even though it's not always with ease
For reminding us the key elements of life
Gratitude and Peace,
It's what we really do this for

Thank You, **M.Muse**
For your honest account
There's blessings coming your way this year
I've told you this, In endless amounts

There's a world for you to explore

Thank You, **Paris Chong**
For keeping romance alive, in a time of where love is hard to
find
It's the simple things
We really need to fly

Thank You, **Morrisson**
For sharing your story
Taking us into the park and the fields
A moment so special, full of love, a bond unbreakable and real
Thank you for sharing a piece of your heart and mind

Thank You, **KSI**
For your honesty and for being so candid
For showcasing to us,
How your experiencing life outside of youtube
In Front of the camera and behind

Thank You, **Olly Williams**
For your beautiful view as to how you see our planet
For breaking down the beauty of wishes, animals, mentors
The last line of your entry hits,
Like magic, my guy!

Thank You, **Sam Tompkins**
For Time Will Fly,
I'm so proud of you Oh My Tompkins
There's always a place for you in my heart
The planet is by your side x

Thank You, **Freddie Pearson**
For sharing wisdom at such an age
For your incredible performance on Invisible
Bringing these words to life from the page
I can't wait to see you on the stage

Thank You, **Ebonee Davis**
For blessing this anthology
With such elegance and powers
 Your words I can read for countless hours
It's a real blessing with you, sharing the page

Thank You, **John Burton**
Not only for your entry
But for everything you have done for me
I miss you on site,
But the memories are strong enough, at my age!

Thank You, **Max Bowden**
For writing, for fighting,
For living, for guiding,
For your will to keep going
And that you always are trying through the grief and pain

Thank You, **Sarah Callaghan**
Honestly, for all your poetry and comedy
It's a blessing to have met you on this creative road
Your smashing it, keep going
Your friend, lovingly Hussain x

Thank You, **Meggan Roxanne**
For surfing along the Healing Waves

Sharing the wisdom and love that your heart has saved
I'm so glad we got to include you in *I Wanted To Quit Too*
Right before the end of the day!

Thank You, **Saida Ahmed**
For your powerful poetry, as it touches spirits
Your talent is boundless, it holds no limits
Thank you for always knowing what to say

Thank You, **Andrea Thompson**
You really did that, the final word
WE STILL MOVE
Andrea, keep going
From your attic bedroom to the world, Okay!!!

Closing Statement: The Brown Room

And here I am, approaching my 33rd birthday, saying goodbye to this book, as it prepares to enter its next phase of life, away from my loyal laptop and into the arms and hearts of those of you who will hopefully welcome it in. The Brown Room, in our family home, is the sacred, forbidden front room, the one room we save for special guests, where the sofas are kept in top condition, the candles never lit, the frames on the wall hang as masterpieces of art. I have found myself here, opening the drawer from the centre table to find special little souvenirs my dear mum kept from my journey. Work badges from Primark, Curry's, Sainsburys, Suits You, the lot. A broken GoPro camera in a waterproof case, the extra Burberry buttons from the new shirt in case one fell off, a microphone clip, a poster from when I headlined Scala in King's Cross, brochures from the Space trip I won that never happened (another story for another day). Sinéad's right, life is a very funny old thing. I left my family home four years ago, eager, excited and unaware of what was in store for me. Returning now, unexpectedly, to my own surprise, I am not sure what brought me back home but something spiritual clearly did at this particular moment and it placed me right here, on the white leather sofas with my feet up (shoes off, of course) in The Brown Room.

I once viewed myself as someone who lost so much in this life, my dear mother, friendships, opportunities, I'd actively seek out issues to justify more reasons to self sabotage, oh and of course, my hair too! But throughout the process of the creation of this book, which I really believe made itself, I also learnt that that is not a healthy mindset for me to have. Hearing these stories made me really reflect. And therefore, I feel like I am doing the much-needed work to become better through all I learnt.

My nephew is one year old, he's in the room next door – we call that The Grey Room. He's calling me to watch him jump around on a small trampoline my sister got him. So before I go, I wanted to say this. I feel so blessed to have been trusted to share the stories that bind this book. And what I have felt throughout this process goes beyond any words that I could ever write. I am truly thankful to everyone who helped me throughout the process to help make this happen. Thank you Murray and Katelyn Cummings, Jay Ellis and Nina Senicar, Nick Jones, James Longman, James Holt and Hira Jagdev and Greg Williams for giving me a place to stay whilst I have been away from home. You welcomed me and took care of me. For that I am eternally grateful. Thank you.

Whilst I am here, Dad, Thank You. Thank you for being so supportive, loving and encouraging. Thank you for always leaving the door open, the lights on and for feeding me and all my friends. I love you Dad. I know, I know, we have a long way to go . . .

Ok, sorry, back to the closing statement! I am still learning. I guess I always will be. And one thing I have learnt is, you know what, sometimes It's alright . . .

*It's alright, if this morning you overslept, and didn't make it to
the gym*

*It's alright, if you missed your appointment, cancelled plans, and
just about opened the curtains feeling the weight of the world as
you pull down on the string*

*It's alright, if you haven't cooked in a while, as you're thinking
what's best to feed your spirit within*

*It's alright, if you can't explain certain feelings, certain thoughts
certain things*

*It's alright, if the shelves have a bit of dust, the corners of the
rooms have got spider webs*

*It's alright, if there's clothes on the floor, and if there's photos
you've turned around by the side of your bed*

*It's alright, if you're thinking you're a mess,
It's alright,
Considering what you've been through,
Considering what you're dealing with
Considering where it's taken you
Considering what is still not making sense*

*It's alright, if you're getting white hair, and a bit of a belly
It's alright, if you sit by yourself on friday night with a portion of
fish and chips, smiling and laughing watching Sekou Diaby kill
scenes on the telly,*

It's alright, and if it's not
It will be, rest, reset, go again once you've recharged
Lighter, smarter,
That little bit brighter
It's alright,

You're not alone, i'm here too
You've got the spirit and soul of a fighter

The little man from The Grey Room is still calling me, so I gotta get a move on, he's lost a sock (it's all kicking off). Being an Uncle is the greatest badge of honour I have been gifted to wear in this lifetime. And being able to spend moments of joy and happiness with my niece and nephews comes both sad and beautiful. It hurts my heart that my dear mother never got this time with her grandchildren.

With that being said, this last one here is for Mum and it's called, 'I Can't Love Like You Could'.

As much as I try to cuddle them in warmth from my jumper
It doesn't match the fabric of your cardigan

I Can't Love Like You Could

As I hide in the kitchen and jump out to scare them
Or blow bubbles whilst teaching them how to dance

I Can't Love Like You Could

Re-building gladiators in the living room with the cushions and
the sofas

I Can Try,
But I Can't Love Like You Could

Telling them stories of their nanny,
So they know, how special she is and how much she loves them

I still, Can't Love Like You Could

Your Nanny, Our Mum, Baba's Wife,

We can all try,
But we can't and we can never
Love Like You Could